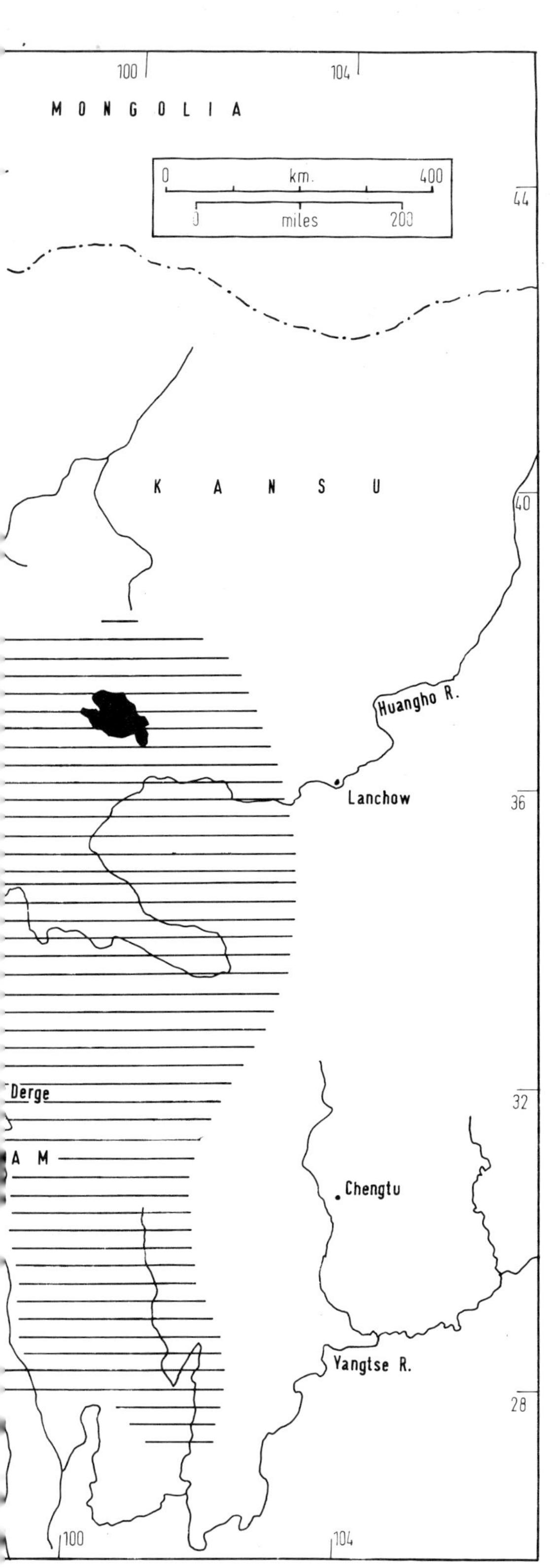
MONGOLIA
km
0
400
miles
200
KANSU
Huangho R.
Lanchow
Derge
A M
Chengtu
Yangtse R.
100
104
44
40
36
32
28

CW00551538

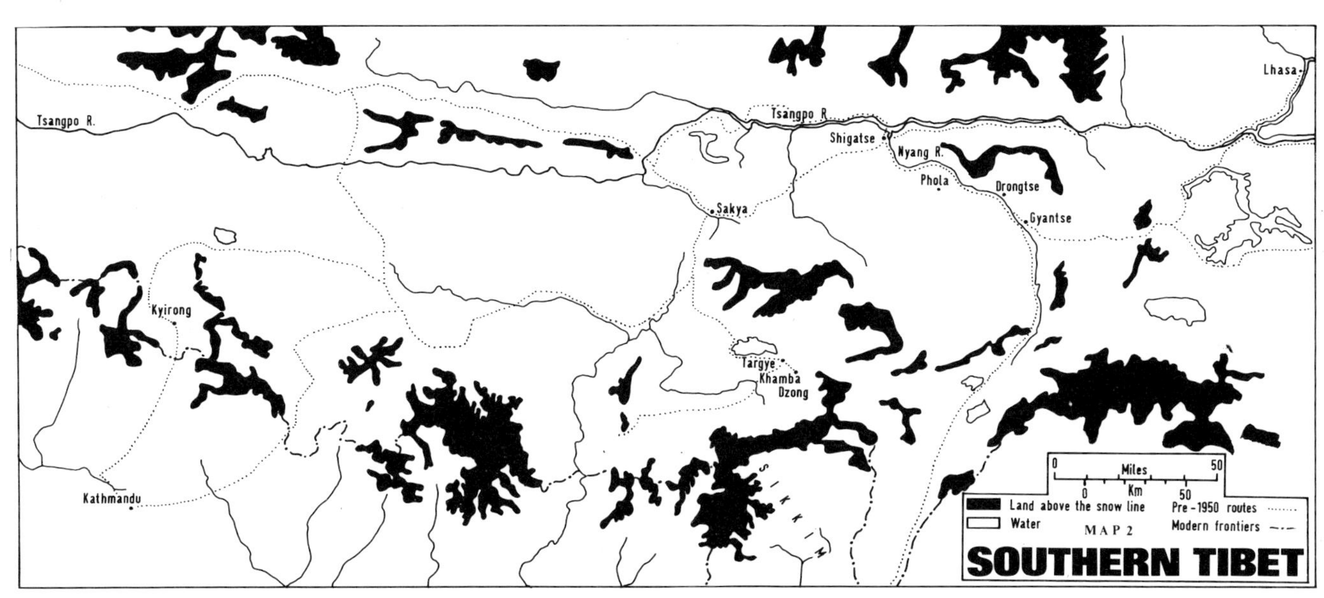
Tsangpo R.
Lhasa
Shigatse
Nyang R.
Phola
Drongtse
Gyantse
Sakya
Kyirong
Targye
Khamba Dzong
Kathmandu
SIKKIM
Miles
Km
0
50
Land above the snow line
Water
Pre-1950 routes
Modern frontiers
MAP 2
SOUTHERN TIBET

THE TIBETAN CARPET

Large Tibetan floor carpet (20′ 6″ × 10′ 4″)
(*Courtesy of Franses of Piccadilly*)

THE TIBETAN CARPET

PHILIP DENWOOD

Aris and Phillips Ltd · Warminster · England

ISBN 0 85668 022 2

Printed in Great Britain by
Biddles Ltd., Guildford, Surrey.

Contents

List of Illustrations

List of Colour Plates

Acknowledgements

Most of the work on which this book is based was done during the winter of 1972–3 in northern India where I was collecting Tibetan books for the library of the School of Oriental and African Studies in the University of London. As my time was limited I was unable to obtain detailed information on the organisation of the carpet industry in pre-1959 Tibet or on the Tibetan conception of carpet design. I have limited myself to presenting a number of illustrations and describing the techniques of manufacture in some detail. Chapter 7 is an attempt to place the Tibetan carpet industry in its geographical and historical setting within the world of oriental carpets.

Many individuals have helped me in collecting and analysing material. I would especially like to thank the following: for the initial inspiration of the book and much cooperation and encouragement, Mr. H. K. Kulöy; for demonstrating weaving techniques to my wife and me, Mr. and Mrs. Lody Gyatsho of the Himalayan Marketing Association and many Tibetan weavers too numerous to mention individually; for helping with the location and photography of carpets, Oppi and Saara Untracht, Dr. David L. Snellgrove, Marilyn Silverstone, the Hon. Mrs. Eric Bailey, Mr. Joseph Gelpie, Mr. Michael Franses, Mr. Simon Matthews of Spink & Son Ltd., Mr. John Lowry of the Victoria and Albert Museum, Mrs. Margaret Warhurst of the Liverpool City Museums, Herr Hans König, Dr. May H. Beattie, Mr. David Tremayne, and Mr. and Mrs. Jack Franses.

Useful advice was given by Marco Pallis who, with the late Aristide Messinesi and others, was among the first to realise the aesthetic merits and technical skill of Tibetan carpets and also established a carpet weaving centre in Kalimpong in the late 1940's.

I would also like to acknowledge with thanks the following for providing illustrations: Dr. David L. Snellgrove (6, 9, 10, 14, 31); The Director of the India Office Library and Records for photographs from the Sir Charles Bell Collection (1, 2, 4, 5, 7, 8, 12, 13, 15, 16, 17, 18, 19, 20, 21a, 21b, 22, 25, 80) and the Col. F. M. Bailey Collection (78); The Royal Geographical Society (11) and Mr. Corneille Jest (58, 59, 60, 61, 62).

Tibetan and sanskrit words in italics are exact transliterations, those between commas are approximate phonetic renderings.

Philip Denwood.
May, 1974.

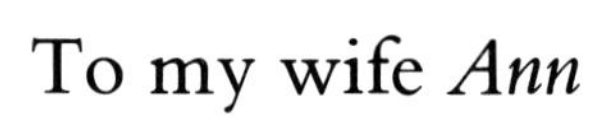

To my wife *Ann*

Introduction

Tibet and the Tibetans[1]

Two regions come to mind when thinking of the word 'Tibet'. I shall call them 'Tibet proper' and 'cultural Tibet'. 'Tibet proper' is a well defined broad geographical unit, and during the 19th and the first half of the 20th centuries it corresponded to the territories controlled by the government of the Dalai Lamas in Lhasa. It is a vast plateau the size of Scandinavia, lying mostly over four thousand metres above sea level. Its northern half is a cold, dry waste of semi-desert, virtually uninhabited. Towards the south this inhospitable zone gradually gives way to rolling steppeland, broken at intervals by wide, shallow river valleys. It is in and around these southern valleys that most of the Tibetans live. The climate here is dry, warm in summer and not too cold in winter. The whole country is crossed by a series of mountain ranges rising above the general level of the plateau. Towards the south-east, some of these ranges converge, leaving between them only narrow gorges through which the headwaters of the Yangtse, Mekong and Salween flow south-eastwards.

1. For readers interested in Tibetan civilisation the works by Snellgrove & Richardson, R. A. Stein, and Tucci are recommended. All contain their own bibliographies. A survey of political events is contained in Shakabpa's book.

Front endpaper: Map II

fig. 1 The outskirts of the town of Gyantse. Preparation of wool and weaving are often carried out on the flat roofs. In the Nyang valley beyond is fertile farming land and some woodland, while the mountains in the distance are fit only for grazing livestock.

fig. 2 Shigatse Dzong (fort), built in the 18th century. In the foreground pilgrims circumambulate sacred 'mani-walls'. The barren terrain is typical of large areas of Tibet.

Front endpaper: Map I

'Cultural Tibet', or 'ethnic Tibet' as it has been called, extends beyond the boundaries of Tibet proper, where peoples of Tibetan stock are settled in the Himalayas and the mountains of western China down to altitudes of about two thousand five hundred metres. It also covers a north-easterly extension of the Tibetan plateau into Amdo and parts of the Kansu province of China. These outlying areas all have one characteristic in common, that although settled by Tibetans, they have not been ruled from the central Tibetan state for the last thousand years. As may be seen from the map, these Tibetans now come under the political ambits of China, India, Nepal, Sikkim, Bhutan, and even Burma. (I exclude the Muslim Baltis of Pakistan, although they speak a form of Tibetan.)

The research for this book was of neccessity undertaken outside Tibet proper, partly in the Himalayas, but mainly among a newly formed extension of 'Cultural Tibet'; the community of refugees who since 1959 have been settled in their thousands at lower altitudes in India, Nepal, Sikkim and Bhutan. Being unable to visit Tibet proper may be no disadvantage as carpet weaving is a minor manifestation of traditional Tibetan culture and as such it probably survives in a more traditional form outside Tibet proper than inside it.

Outline of Cultural History

The Tibetans are a distinctive group of peoples who share a common body of customs and beliefs, or who did so up to 1959. They are a racially diverse people with a strong mongoloid strain. Their language being ultimately related to Chinese, is akin to several others which are spoken in the Himalayas and to Burmese.

Before the 7th century AD nothing is known of the Tibetans, except perhaps a little from stray pieces of information in Chinese sources which describe western tribes of uncertain identity. Linguistic and literary evidence suggests that the Tibetans originated somewhere on the eastern fringes of present-day Tibet, where they were probably in contact with other ethnic groups, some of them speakers of other closely related Tibeto-Burman languages. From these eastern parts they spread westwards at some unknown date, to found in the 7th century a powerful kingdom centred on the Yarlung valley in southern Tibet. The kingdom was welded together largely by King Songtsen Gampo (c. 609–649 AD) and by his father before him, out of a series of petty chiefdoms, most of them occupying a single valley controlled from a fortress. The power of the kings very quickly expanded to cover all the areas now occupied by Tibetan-speaking groups, and indeed far beyond them to include at various times between the 7th and 9th centuries, Nepal, parts of northern India, much of the Tarim Basin (now Chinese Turkestan or East Turkestan) and parts of western China. The area covered by Tibetan culture was extended both by the settlement of Tibetans in new territories and by the 'Tibetanising' of other groups of people—a process which has gone on in a greater or lesser degree down to the present day. During this period of about two centuries the Tibetans came into active contact, whether as settlers, traders, raiders or conquerors, with Indians, Nepalese, Iranian and Turkish speakers in Central Asia, and with Chinese. They were probably in touch with the late Sasanian empire of Persia and certainly met the armies of the advancing Arabs.

The most obvious cultural result of these two centuries of contact with surrounding peoples was the introduction of Mahayana Buddhism, the common cultural denominator of the areas all round Tibet. Doubtless many other beliefs and practices were imported during the same period from China, Iran and Central Asia. In its essentials, however, Tibetan material culture seems to have been much the same in the 7th century as it has been ever since, which indicates that any large-scale cultural borrowing apart from Buddhism took place at some earlier date. That there was such borrowing is suggested by the many similarities between Tibet and western Asia in such spheres as farming systems and domestic architecture.

Tibetan architecture in particular is evidently a variety of the general western Asiatic type, based on a combination of heavy load-bearing walls with wooden columns and capitals. This architecture was widespread in western Asia from about the 4th millennium BC, and was exemplified in all the great civilisations of the Near and Middle East. The Tibetans evidently acquired it before the development of the arch, as did the Indians, and in many structural and decorative details their use of architecture recalls the styles of Achemenid Persia. Some of these styles seem also to have survived in another mountainous centre of civilisation, the Caucasus, where peculiar multi-storeyed and towerlike buildings very like those of the Tibetans were perhaps first developed. There are other clues such as fragments of folklore, funeral customs and some early religious ideas which point to early connections between Tibet and the west, but it is impossible to tell in the present state of our knowledge whether, and if so when, these cultural traits were borrowed from neighbouring peoples or whether they were taken over from some pre-existing population on the Tibetan plateau. The design of the Tibetan nomads' black tents is also clearly western, though the white tents with awnings used by settled Tibetans seem to be derived from China. Most Tibetan clothing, especially the sewn, belted coats of wool and the felt boots, belongs to the Central Asian world, for similar garments are worn by Mongols and other Central Asian peoples.

fig. 3 A small farming village in Tsang province.

The contacts suggested by all these items seem to be very ancient. Indian influence, on the other hand, is clearly traceable to historical times—the 7th century on—and is almost all associated with the importation of Buddhism. Before that time it is doubtful whether the Tibetans had much if any contact with the classical Indian civilisation which lay beyond the Himalayas. From perhaps as early as the 9th century down to the demise of Buddhism in India in the 13th, the Buddhist religion was by far the most dominant outside influence exerted on Tibet. The whole culture which grew up around it in Tibet was vigorously maintained and developed until 1959 in Tibet proper, and still survives in somewhat fragmentary form in various parts of the Himalayas. Indian Mahayana Buddhism gave the Tibetans their principal religious ideas and practices as well as a whole range of art forms: scroll and mural painting, woodcarving and metalwork, styles of religious dress, architectural decoration, liturgical music, ritual dances, popular oral and written literature. So thoroughly were these spheres of activity transformed under Buddhist influence that it is often hard to distinguish any non-Buddhist elements within them. Buddhism pervaded the very fabric of Tibetan life to a degree known in few other countries.

In the mid 9th century, while this cultural process was getting under way, the Tibetan empire suddenly collapsed. Most of its territories which were occupied by non-Tibetan peoples were lost for ever. The Tibetan-populated areas split up into a number of petty principalities, many of which were reunited in the 13th century under the aegis of the Mongols. This reunited territory substantially constituted what I have termed 'Tibet proper'. It has been ruled for most of the time since then by religious hierarchs of one or other of the orders of Tibetan Buddhism—since the 17th century by the Dalai Lamas who have headed the Gelugpa or Yellow Hat order. The past six centuries have seen few major changes in Tibetan culture apart from a steady proliferation throughout the country of monasteries which have housed in modern times a sizeable fraction of the male population—perhaps as high as 20% in some areas, though probably not more than 10% in most.

Soon after Tibet's reunification in the 13th century, Buddhism became all but extinct in India, and the Tibetans ceased to look in that direction for anything but trade; the exchange of wool, salt and skins against Indian grain, dyestuffs and cotton. Henceforth what outside cultural influence there was on Tibet came from Mongolia and China. From the Mongols the Tibetans borrowed some administrative methods, official titles and articles of clothing. The use of tea and silk imported from China was already well established by the 11th century. By the 15th century the Tibetans had adopted Chinese methods of paper-making and printing from wooden blocks, although they modelled their books on the Indian format. The strength of Chinese political influence on Tibet waxed and waned with internal conditions in China and with the changes in the fortunes of their main rivals in Central Asia, the Mongols. It was strongest in the last three-quarters of the 18th century under the Manchus, who claimed a form of protectorate over Tibet and who lavishly patronised Tibetan Buddhism. At that time there is a noticeable, if superficial, influence exerted by Chinese artistic styles and aesthetics on Tibetan tastes. Although very few of the Tibetan aristocracy ever learned Chinese or took any genuine interest in Chinese culture, some of their manners became increasingly sinicised, most notably in some of their styles of dress and some of their cookery. The demand grew for a few easily transported Chinese luxury products; principally fine porcelain cups and bowls, and brocade silks. The use of Chinese porcelain and brocade has by now filtered down to the middle levels of Tibetan society, though it has by no means driven out native products. A family which on some festive occasion eats quasi-Chinese food with chopsticks out of Chinese bowls may for everyday use revert to Tibetan roasted barley-flour eaten with the fingers from home-produced wooden cups. Chinese products, including carpets on occasion were thus imported mainly as luxuries, with the important exception of tea which has for centuries been drunk at most levels of the population.

The large monasteries used quantities of Chinese silk for certain types of ceremonial dress. Some Chinese architectural motifs were applied to Tibetan monastic buildings, without much regard to their original functions, while some styles of religious painting were noticeably influenced by Chinese landscape and figure styles. Some of these Chinese cultural influences go back to Ming times or even earlier, but they certainly received a strong impetus under the Manchus.

During the first three decades of the 20th century, Tibet's continued isolation from the rest of the world ensured that no major cultural influences came from outside. After 1905 there was increased trading and other contact with British India which led to the introduction of a few western products. Some Indian-manufactured goods became available in greater quantities in the main bazaars, but the use of western-style products such as high tables and chairs, cameras and window glass hardly became more than an eccentric fad indulged in by a few aristocratic families. Tibetan life continued much as before, aesthetic preferences still being for the existing bland of indigenous Tibetan, Indian and Chinese styles, at least down to the 1930s. Even after 1940 the introduction of foreign products was slow by Asian standards, and outside Lhasa and the main trading centres they still had virtually no impact on traditional ways of life.

fig. 4 A high-ranking Tibetan nobleman of the Phalha family poses for a formal photograph. His Chinese-style dress contrasts with the simple Tibetan clothes of his attendants. The carpet has a design with auspicious emblems.

Ways of life[2]

Most Tibetans are farmers, living in substantial houses among their fields in the river valleys where there is enough water to grow crops. The farmhouses are of two or more storeys, built of stone, mud brick or rammed earth, usually with flat roofs. Livestock—cattle, goats and donkeys—are quartered on the ground floor, with storerooms above them and the family living quarters often in a higher storey still. The roof is used for storing fuel and fodder, and as an extension of the living space. Around the houses are the small fields, fed with water through systems of narrow channels and embankments from some spring or reservoir. In most places a single crop of barley, wheat, buckwheat, potatoes, roots or peas is all that can be grown in a year, and the harvest must be stored in the houses for the long winter. On the whole, the pattern of existence and the means of livelihood are similar to those found in many upland parts of Afghanistan and Iran.

The vast stretches of steppe and mountain lying between these cultivable valleys are used by the valley-dwelling farmers, and by by small bands of nomadic tent-dwelling pasturalists, for grazing sheep, cattle and yak. The nomads rely for survival on the produce of their sheep and yak, principally wool, meat and milk, some of which they may exchange for grain with the farmers. They move around their well-defined territories on horseback, living in black tents which are very like those used by certain Iranian and Arab nomads. Some Tibetans manage to combine the two modes of life—settled farming and nomadism—either by practising them at different times of year or by dividing the different tasks among themselves. Almost all Tibetans like to travel long distances occasionally in pursuit of trade, religion, pleasure or all three.

2. The works by Carrasco, Cassinelli & Ekvall, may be consulted for information on the economic and social conditions in various parts of Tibet.

fig. 5 The wife of the man in Fig. 4. She wears the Tsang style of head-dress.

fig. 6 A group of Tibetan nomads and their tent.

Traditionally, monasteries and aristocratic households were the main nuclei of wealth and sophisticated culture. Most valleys would have one or more monasteries as well as a few estates held by noble families.

The houses on these estates, though large, were essentially overgrown farmhouses, run on similar lines but on a bigger and more lavish scale. Usually each valley was overlooked by the local governor's fort or 'dzong', a strongpoint where the surplus grain of the district was stored. Urban life was poorly developed—indeed scarcely existent outside Lhasa, itself a town of modest size. Apart from Lhasa, and Gyantse and Shigatse in Tsang province, most 'towns' were simply overgrown monasteries or trade marts of fluctuating size.

After farming and animal herding, the most important source of income has always been trade. Petty traders, many of them farmers or members of farming families, distributed the surplus produce of different regions through a complex system of local trading connections. Monasteries and wealthy traders also played a part. Considerable amounts of wool, salt, borax, hides and musk were exported in exchange for manufactures beyond the scope of Tibetans—especially porcelain and silk—and for foodstuffs in short supply. such as grain, or which would not grow in Tibet, such as tea. Most ordinary household goods such as clothing, tools, farm equipment, pots, utensils and so forth, were made locally. Tibetans were and are versatile craftsmen and craftswomen, as the 18th century Italian missionary Ippolito Desideri testified:-

'By nature the Thibettans are seldom idle or lazy but generally occupied with something. Indeed one may say they are more or less skilled in all things necessary for every-day life; such as spinning, weaving, sewing, making ropes, curing hides, mending boots, doing carpentry, building, making paper or powder, cooking, working on the land and tending animals, making butter and cheese, in short they can do nearly everything needful for a family or a house.'[3]

3. See Desideri, p. 186.

Chapter One
Tibetans and their Carpets

The Tibetan use of Carpets

Unlike the Persian or Turk, who has often covered the walls and floor of his house or tent with carpets, the Tibetan uses his carpet mainly as a seat or bed. Carpets come into the category of *gdan*—'seats'.[1] The word, also used to translate the Sanskrit *āsana*, 'seat', is often used alone to refer to a carpet, which for the Tibetan is the typical form of seat. Inside the living rooms on the top storey of the Tibetan farmhouse, furnishings are sparse and practical. Cooking is done on a stove of baked clay, which releases plenty of smoke into the room as no chimneys are provided, only windows and perhaps a hole in the roof.

1. Dictionaries list a word *stan* meaning much the same as *gdan*. I have not heard it used colloquially.

fig. 7 A Tibetan lama seated on a carpet of geometrical design on a raised platform at the side of his room.

fig. 8 A nobleman's retainer on horseback. The horse's lower saddle-cloth is made of woven material, its upper one is a knotted carpet.

fig. 9 The headman of Dolpo, a Tibetan-speaking area of northwest Nepal. His saddle rests on a large lower saddle carpet.

Pots, pans and other cooking implements are ranged on hooks and shelves on the walls, and most other possessions stored away in chests and boxes. There may be a few low tables, but no chairs; people sit crosslegged on mats, blankets or carpets which may be spread over thick paliasses or layers of felt. These in turn may be laid on low wooden platforms around the edges of the rooms, or else simply on the earthen or wooden floor. The same resting-places serve as beds by night. For everyday use, any fine carpets will probably be turned upside down or covered with cloths to protect them from dirt and soot. The carpets, with their underlying padding, can easily be moved onto the roof or into a courtyard by anyone who wishes to sit outside in sunny weather, or they can be transported any distance to the site of a picnic, which is a favourite form of Tibetan diversion. At the picnic spot the carpets will be spread on the ground under awnings or marquees. Similar tents were traditionally used by wealthy Tibetans for their nightly halts when travelling, and the carpets would go with them. This agreeable mode of travelling is still preferred in Bhutan by anyone able to afford it.

fig. 10 A Tibetan couple from Tsang province, residing in Khumbu , a Tibetan-speaking (Sherpa) region of Nepal, who earn their living by carpet-weaving. They sit on a small knotted carpet over a large looped carpet of simple design.

Carpets of some sort will also be found inside the nomad's tent, as they are a convenient, transportable bedding. Those in the poorer tents may be coarse and rough, but the wealthier nomads will use the finest carpets. In monasteries also, the monks will normally sit on carpets, again usually over some kind of mattress. A monk's cell is equipped with a low platform for the carpet, in front of which is a low table for resting a book. In the chapels and temple halls where communal ceremonies are held, cushions, covered with carpets, are laid out in rows. Lamas of high rank generally sit on higher platforms or piles of cushions, as befits their more elevated status, but still in a crosslegged position and on a carpet.

Even when riding, the Tibetan sits on a carpet, or sometimes on a pair of carpets, one under the saddle and one over it, which act as

fig. 11 The abbot of Khamba Dzong, photographed in his tent by John Claude White (1905). Thick mattresses are used as seats. The carpet in the foreground is not Tibetan but from Chinese Turkestan.

saddle cloths. While ordinary carpets are square or oblong, rarely more than six feet long, saddle carpets are often distinctively shaped, tapering towards one side.

Tibetans certainly use floor carpets on occasion, that is, carpets left in place of the floor and walked upon, and sometimes hang carpets on the walls, over doors, and even on the ceiling. Another curious use should be mentioned—the custom of enveloping the pillars of temples with special cylindrical carpets, which seems to have been commonest in the areas most influenced by China. However, the vast majority of Tibetan carpets were made and used as seats, which is why they are often most worn in the middle, and as beds. Tibetan refugees in India still cover their beds with carpets, for the standard six foot by three carpet they now make covers an Indian charpoy bed exactly.

The Distribution of the Craft

The regional spread of carpet weaving in Tibet is only sketchily known. I suspect that carpets and rugs of one sort or another were made in most areas where Tibetan-speaking peoples lived, though most of my informants from eastern Tibet, Kham and Amdo, profess total ignorance of carpet weaving and do not remember seeing it practised in their

fig. 12 Carpet weaving at Penjor Lhunpo (Drongtse) 1933.

fig. 13 Carpet weaving at Penjor Lhunpo (Drongtse) 1933.

native districts. Nevertheless others claim to have seen it there and carpets were certainly used and traded in those regions. The most active carpet weaving area, and that from which the best carpets came, was undoubtedly the southern province of Tsang. Many a farmer's wife from Tsang could produce a serviceable carpet along with her homespun cloth, woven from wool which she had probably carded, spun and dyed herself. Such occupations were mainly winter work, and the resulting carpets would be for use in her own household or for selling locally. The richer households of Tsang sometimes numbered among their retainers several weavers, employed from time to time in replacing worn carpets, and the local governors in this province often had teams of weavers—men and women—producing carpets for sale

fig. 14 The weaver of Fig. 10 at work.

to monasteries or wealthy individuals. After the trade agreement with British India in 1904, some carpets were exported to India, mainly from these larger workshops. A few traders in places like Kyirong took an interest in the possibilities and sponsored extra manufacture of carpets. In the early part of this century and up to 1959, organised workshops producing good quality carpets were operating at Gyantse, Shigatse, Sakya, Kyirong and Khampa Dzong to my knowledge and there were probably small concerns at many other places in the region. Sarat Chandra Das mentions rug weaving at Targye, Gyantse and near Phola in the 1880s. None of this activity was on a large scale by non-Tibetan standards as probably no workshop employed more than twenty or thirty weavers, and the majority of production was for immediate local use. There is little information on the organisation of the craft. Carpet weaving was a fairly lowly occupation, most weavers being simple farmers' wives or servants.

fig. 15 Carpets for sale in Gyantse market, 1933.

Tibetan nomads supplied much of the best wool for carpet weaving, but except for some groups in western Tibet they seem to have played little or no part in the actual manufacture. A few Tsang families became renowned for their skill and traditions and specialised in the weaving of fine carpets of the overseeing of workshops, thereby earning a respectable living from carpet weaving alone. As for quality, most Tibetans put Gyantse in the first place, though just as good carpets were probably made in Shigatse.

The valley of the Nyang river between Gyantse and Shigatse, which includes the district of Panam, may be regarded as the centre of the Tibetan carpet industry for both quality and quantity. It is by all accounts a pleasant, prosperous stretch of country, heavily populated by Tibetan standards, scattered with farming villages. There were a number of monasteries large and small, several forts and some noble estates. Sheep, famed for their high-quality wool, were kept both on the neighbouring uplands and in the valley itself, which was well-known also for its woollen broadcloths and serges.

The craft also flourished in parts of the central province of Ü, for instance in and around Lhasa where there was a sizeable demand for good carpets. Aristocratic households might have their own weavers or buy from small workshops. In the western province of Ngari the craft was widespread on a village level and was even practised by some nomads, though there seems to have been little or no production for sale. In the Himalayan regions the weaving of simple carpets has been observed in Ladakh, some of the Bhotia regions of the Indian Himalayas and Sikkim, and in some of the Tibetan-speaking valleys of northern Nepal. Carpet weaving probably still goes on in most of the Tibetan-speaking Himalayas from Ladakh to Sikkim, but I have not so far traced any record of it in Bhutan (except among recently arrived Tibetan refugees). It is practised by the Monpas and others of the North East Frontier Agency (NEFA). The kings of Sikkim have during this century supported workshops making fine carpets.

The distribution pattern is one of simple carpet weaving as a common village craft over most of the centre, west and south of the Tibetan cultural area, becoming more organised and sophisticated in a very few urban or semi-urban centres within this region. To the east, northeast and southeast it was of far less importance, and apparently totally absent in most districts.

Since 1959 there has been no information about carpet weaving in 'Autonomous' Tibet, except for the news that the Chinese authorities have set up a carpet factory in Lhasa. This was visited in 1962 by Stuart and Roma Gelder, and seems to have been something similar to a modern refugee carpet workshop, but headed by a Chinese manager. The recent social upheavals in Tibet have doubtless disrupted the old pattern of the craft, but how far it has been reestablished on new lines, as has happened to the carpet industry in China proper, we do not know. Among Tibetan refugees in India, Nepal, Sikkim and Bhutan the craft has proved a valuable source of income and has taken on a new lease of activity.

Chapter Two
Materials

Traditional Sources for the Materials

Before the first world war most of the materials for Tibetan carpets were home produced. The warp, weft and pile of the carpet were all made from Tibetan wool. Dyestuffs were made from plants and minerals found in Tibet, with the important exceptions of indigo, imported from India and perhaps China, and lac, imported from India and Bhutan. Cotton cloth for backing the carpets was also imported. Mordants, scouring agents and other substances used in preparing the wool were locally produced.

Recent changes

The use of new materials during the present century has resulted in a complete change in the texture and quality of many Tibetan carpets, although they remain characteristically Tibetan in design. Increasing trade contacts with India between the wars quickly led to the importation of cotton yarn for use as warp threads. The main reason for this was probably that cotton was cheaper than wool, though it is true that a cotton warp does provide a more stable basis for a carpet, being less subject to unpredictable and differential shrinkage than wool. By the 1950s, most carpets had cotton warp threads, but wool was only just starting to give way to cotton for the weft threads. Even today, a few carpets are produced with woollen wefts. The most noticeable effect of cotton warps and wefts is that the finished carpet is much stiffer and rather less soft and resilient.

Along with cotton, the Tibetans also began to import synthetic dyestuffs. Again, cheapness was a factor in their increasing use, but Tibetans seem to have liked the lighter, more vivid colours obtainable with their aid. Over the past century, Tibetan taste as a whole has swung over from subtle colour schemes which blended together both bright and sombre shades, to much lighter, brighter compositions which often appear garish to Western eyes. The immediate result of synthetic dyes was to increase the range and variety of the colours in Tibetan carpets. A carpet which previously had only four or five harmonising vegetable colours might now have anything up to sixteen synthetic shades, not always well chosen. Natural dyestuffs are still widely used in Bhutan, and although the Bhutanese do not weave carpets themselves, they do supply some natural dyestuffs to the few Tibetan refugee settlements which still take the trouble to use them. Madder, rhubarb, vegetable indigo, myrabolan and barberry are still readily obtainable in Darjeeling, and local Tibetans make use of them. Most refugee carpet workshops have however gone over completely to Indian-produced synthetic dyes, occasionally doing their own dyeing but more often buying their yarn ready dyed.

fig. 16 Wool being transported by yak.

fig. 17 Tibetan sheep in the Nyang valley.

Wool

Information on Tibetan sheep may be found in the works by Epstein, Ekvall and Mason mentioned in the bibliography. There are at least two distinct types of sheep in Tibet; a large, long-legged breed mainly found in the north of the country, whose fleece may contain 25% or more of hair, kept by the nomads; and a shorter-legged, less hairy breed kept by the valley-dwelling farmers. Probably both types vary from place to place. The wool may in its natural state be white, brown or black. In comparison with other wools, Tibetan wool is coarse, hairy, long-stapled, very lustrous, and of high tensile strength. It is in fact the ideal carpet wool, being strong, springy, and flexible. Its high lustre and the presence of hair give the pile a distinct sheen when viewed from certain angles. It takes natural dyes well—subtlety is imparted to the colours by the presence of hairs which take up less dye than do the wool fibres, while the lustre gives the colours depth and life. Tibetan wools are still used by refugees in Nepal, and a few settlements in the Himalayas can buy mountain wool of qualities similar to the Tibetan, but elsewhere among refugees, lowland Indian wool has to be used. This, though it makes a hard-wearing floor carpet, is decidedly inferior aesthetically to Tibetan wool, in comparison with which it is weak, lacking in springiness and flexibility, and dull in appearance, especially when coloured, as it usually is, with synthetic dyes.[1]

fig. 18 Carding wool at Penjor Lhunpo (Drongtse) 1933.

It is common in areas of traditional Tibetan culture to see both men and women spinning wool as they walk about, using a simple hanging spindle. Spinning is said also to be done by rolling the wool with the hand on the thigh. Sometimes the tip of the spindle is rested in a small clay or metal cup on the ground. Sir Charles Bell photographed hand-powered spinning wheels in use in Tsang province in the 1930s. Such wheels are still used by refugees for reeling yarn. Wool for weft

1. Woollen yarn ready for use is generally called *spun-dog* ('pündok').

fig. 19 Spinning wool with a simple spindle which rests in a potsherd (Drongtse 1933).

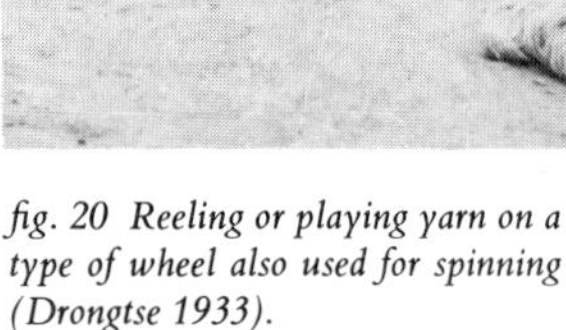

fig. 20 Reeling or playing yarn on a type of wheel also used for spinning (Drongtse 1933).

threads is spun loosely into yarn of about $\frac{1}{8}''$ in diameter, and for warp threads much tighter into yarn of about $\frac{1}{16}''$ in diameter. Pile yarn is spun to a diameter of about $\frac{1}{8}''$ and is often used double. Most woollen yarns which I have examined closely—whether for warp, weft or pile—have proved to be 'S-spun'—that is, with the spindle whorl rotating clockwise.

Cotton

Little need be said about the cotton yarn now generally used for both warp and weft threads. It is mill spun to about $\frac{1}{16}''$ in diameter, being in effect ordinary string. It is not always of high quality—the thickness may fluctuate markedly.

Camel Hair and Yak Hair

Camel hair was occasionally used for the pile of carpets in Tibet. Imported from Mongolia or northern Tibet, it gives a fine, smooth pile. Yak hair was used to weave tent cloth by the nomads and sometimes for woven, non-pile carpets or mats, such as the common yak hair blankets of Bhutan.

Dyestuffs

As well as undyed wool—white, brown or black— the Tibetans have traditionally incorporated dyed wool into their carpets. Three generalisations which hold good for the dyer's craft in traditional societies throughout most of the old world certainly apply to Tibet. Firstly, the craft is, or was, a 'mystery'; a complicated, semi-secret and often hereditary art, transmitted by example and word of mouth. It is therefore difficult for the outsider to investigate. Secondly, it was dependant on a small number of well-known, tried and tested dyestuffs which were important in international commerce, principally indigo, madder and red insect dyes (lac in the case of Tibet). Thirdly, these dyestuffs were supplemented by a wide range of local materials of varying reliability, usually vegetable but sometimes animal or mineral. A few of those used by Tibetans are walnut, rhubarb, barberry, myrobalan, buckwheat and tea. The effectiveness of dyes from this group varies with the local soil and climate and with the dyer's skill, but usually they are not so fast as those of the previously mentioned group.

No study in depth has yet been made of Tibetan dyeing, but the little information I was able to collect is set out below. It all applies to recent times.[2]

2. Identification of Tibetan plant and mineral names, of which many are recorded, can rarely be 100% certain. The present generation of Tibetans is probably the last to retain a knowledge of the vernacular names. There is a large Tibetan medical literature, some of which can be related to Sanskrit, Chinese, Khotanese or Mongol texts, but no-one has yet undertaken the difficult and specialised task of making systematic cross-identifications of plants and minerals. I hope to give the reasons behind my own identifications in a separate publication.

For information on natural dyestuffs in general I have relied fairly heavily on Rawson, Gardner & Laycock. Other important works on the subject are listed in the bibliography.

Indigo

Indigo (Tibetan *ram* or *rams*) was imported from India in processed form. Most Tibetan dyers seem to be unaware that it comes or came from a plant, though it is known as such in the medical texts, and a word denoting the indigo plant is found in some dictionaries. The subtropical plants (chiefly *Indigofera tinctoria*) from which it is extracted have been grown in India for at least two thousand years, and perhaps for as long in China. In the 19th century *Indigofera tinctoria* was grown on a massive scale in Bihar and Bengal on British-run plantations, and processed there for export. Although the industry virtually died out there in the early 20th century, the plant is still grown in South India. A plant known as *rams* and yielding a blue dye is still grown in Bhutan—this is probably not *Indigofera tinctoria* but some other plant containing indigotin. Other indigotin-bearing plants have been grown in China.

fig. 21a Carpet weaving at Penjor Llunpo (Drongtse) 1933. The boy is grinding indigo.

The Tibetans used to import most of their indigo from India in the form of small dried cakes or blocks—an account of how these were produced may be found in *A Dictionary of Dyes* by Rawson, Gardner and Laycock. The Tibetans then ground up these cakes very thoroughly in a mortar with a little vegetable oil or water, to make a paste whose active constituent was indigotin. Before being applied to the yarn indigotin has to be reduced to 'indigo white', which is done according to one Tibetan recipe by mixing it with rhubarb juice and standing it to ferment. The reduction is performed by one of the constituents of rhubarb, oxalic acid (a powerful reducing agent) and/or by the products of fermentation. In another recipe the indigotin is mixed with Tibetan beer which is still fermenting. The paste may take several days to grind and several more to ferment. The resulting brew, with water added, is warmed to a critical temperature well below boiling point (about 55 degrees centigrade, if European experience is anything to go by) for steeping the yarn. The blue colour develops on the yarn by reoxidisation as it is drying. Subsequent steepings of fresh yarn in the same liquid will give successively lighter shades of blue. These the Tibetans especially value, no doubt because they have no other source of the colour.

Areas dyed with indigo on Tibetan carpets often have an uneven, streaky appearance, patches of lighter and darker blue being mingled together. This is because the Tibetans cannot make their wool take this dye as evenly as other colours.

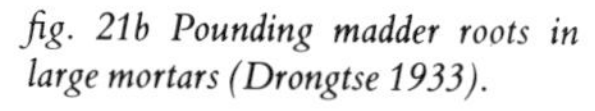
fig. 21b Pounding madder roots in large mortars (Drongtse 1933).

Madder

Madder (Tibetan *btsod*) produces various shades of red, often of a purplish cast. The name is given to several closely related plants of the genus *Rubia*. Most Indian madder is said to be obtained from *Rubia munjista* (*cordifolia*) alleged to contain only the colouring matter

fig. 22 Soaking woven cloth in a dyebath of madder (Drongtse 1933).

purpurin, giving a duller shade than dyes prepared from *R. tinctoria* and *R. peregrina*, formerly grown in Europe and the U.S.A. These two species contain much more alizarin than purpurin, and the Tibetans may have used one or both of them, since their imports came from the Himalayas. There is a Himalayan species, *R. sikkimensis*. Madder is still produced in Sikkim, Bhutan and north-east Nepal. The Tibetans also grew it themselves in the warmer parts of Tsang province. Of the following four recipes for dyeing with madder, the first was certainly used in Tibet for dyeing wool, the other three for silk and cotton, and perhaps also wool:

1. The yarn is first boiled in a solution of a mineral called *dmartshur* (probably an alumaceous earth) which serves as a mordant. This colours it a yellow ochre or buff shade. The mixture must be boiled on until it is no longer sour to the taste. The yarn is taken out and while still wet is sprinkled with powdered madder root. It is then boiled in fresh water until the required shade of dullish red is obtained. The spent madder is washed off the yarn, which is again reboiled in the same water to which sodium carbonate (*bul-tog*) has been added. It is finally washed and dried. The same madder may be used to dye further batches of yarn successively lighter shades. The process is in accord with western methods of dyeing with madder using alum mordant and often chalk or another alkali in the place of sodium carbonate.

2. Having been well washed, the yarn is boiled in milk, and then dried in the sun. It is then mordanted by boiling it in a solution of *spang-tshur*, probably copper sulphate, or alternatively in the juice of an unidentified plant and then dried again. Finally it is boiled together

with the madder, though apparently with the flowers this time, not the roots. If a vivid shade of red is needed a further dipping in a solution of borax or sour beer is carried out. The borax provides the required alkali, but the function of the milk and beer is not clear.

3. The yarn is simply boiled in milk, dried, and reboiled with madder, to produce a dull red shade.

4. The yarn is first washed in the juice of a plant known as *sug-pa,* probably soapwort (*Saponaria officinalis*) or a related plant, and then mordanted by being boiled in copper sulphate. It is then dyed according to one of the above three methods.

Lac-dye

Lac-dye (Tibetan *rgya-skegs*—the resulting colour is known as *rgya-tshos*) is employed by Tibetans to give reds, usually of a scarlet type. It is the oriental equivalent of the kermes and cochineal colours used in the Middle East and Europe, being derived from the egg-sacs of *Coccus lacca* or closely related insects which live on the bark of certain Indian and Burmese trees, notably *Butea frondosa*, the Bastard Teak or Butea Gum. The female insects extract the dyestuff from the tree, together with a resin (shellac), glueing themselves to the twigs with a hard incrustation. The encrusted twigs, when broken off, are known as stick-lac, and it was in this form that lac was imported into Tibet from Assam and eastern Bhutan. The Tibetans extracted the dye by crushing the stick-lac into small pieces and boiling it in water to which are added the leaves of an unidentified plant (possibly a rhododendron, or *Symplocos racemosa,* the Lodh tree). I have no information on Tibetan methods of dyeing with the resulting liquid, but in Persia and India it is boiled with the yarn which has previously been mordanted by boiling or soaking in a solution of alum. From the residue of the stick-lac the Tibetans extracted a reddish wax used by metalworkers and as sealing wax.

Rhubarb

Rhubarb is the Tibetans' chief source of yellow dye, and its pressed juice is often used as an ingredient in dye baths with other dyestuffs. The leaves are known as *cho-lo* and the roots as *chu-rtsa*. Various species of *Rheum* have been suggested—probably the Tibetans used different species in different places. A yellow colour is produced by boiling the yarn with dried rhubarb leaves, the addition of *ser-tshur* resulting in a more golden shade. From the roots a bright orange-brown colour is obtained—the roots are dried, powdered and boiled with the yarn.

Walnut[3]

The walnut tree, some species of *Juglans*, provides the Tibetans' chief brown dye. It is also used widely for this purpose in Persia. Walnuts are cultivated in the warmer parts of western, central and southern Tibet. The usual method of preparation of the dye is to leave the husks of unripe walnuts to rot in water, for some months if necessary. They are then dried and powdered. In dyeing, the yarn is simply boiled up

3. Some interesting information on the history of the walnut in Asia is given in Laufer, pp. 254ff. There are also sections on saffron and turmeric, safflower, henna, indigo, oak-galls, myrobalan and other relevant commodities.

together with the powder as no mordant is required. Different shades of brown are obtained by altering the degree of acidity of the dye bath, which is done by adding rhubarb juice (oxalic acid) or sodium carbonate. Similar recipes using walnuts are known from Europe.

Combinations of Dyes

To produce intermediate shades and secondary colours on the yarn, combinations of two or more of the above-mentioned dyestuffs may be used. Usually the yarn is dyed in the different dyestuffs successively, and dried in between. Thus light green, for example, is obtained by redyeing, with indigo, yarn already dyed with rhubarb. Madder and lac are often combined to give different shades of red. Careful dyers will go to great lengths to achieve the exact shade required, if necessary by dyeing and redyeing many times over. The main disadvantage of this practice is that large quantities of wood which is scarce in Tibet are used in heating the dye baths.

Other Dyestuffs

Many other substances are mentioned by informants or in texts as being used for dyeing, though all are not necessarily used for dyeing carpet wool. They include the following:-

Barberry (*Berberis asiatica*, Tibetan *skyer-pa*)—a thorny shrub common in the Himalayas, whose bark and wood give a bright yellow dye. No mordant is required. This dyestuff is sometimes confused with turmeric.

Rumex (sorrel or dock—precise species unknown—Tibetan *sho-mang*)—a plant similar to rhubarb, but growing in lower-lying places, and smaller. It is unusual in giving a light green dye from its leaves.

Buckwheat (*Fagopyrum esculentum*—Tibetan *bra'u*)—grown by the Tibetans as a food crop, and yields a yellow dye from its leaves and seeds. It may also be used to darken the colours produced by other dyestuffs.

Larch or pine (Tibetan *thang-shing*—probably a range of different species)—the young green cones may be crushed and dried, after which they may be stored for long periods. They give a greenish or bluish colour.

Polygonum (species unknown—Tibetan *snya-lo*)—the flowers, boiled and strained, yield a liquid which dyes green. This may be *Polygonum tinctorium*.

Turmeric (a species of *Curcuma*,—Tibetan *yung-ba* or *yung-nga*)—the tubers or rhizomes of this widely cultivated Indian culinary plant, when powdered, may be used in the same dye bath as rhubarb root for a yellow-orange colour.

Safflower (*Carthamus tinctoria*—Tibetan *gur-gum*)—cultivated in Kashmir, gives red and orange colours formerly used for dyeing monks' robes. A variety of it was grown in Tibet. The Tibetans, like many others, often confuse this dyestuff with saffron (*Crocus sativus*). Sometimes the two were mixed together.

Myrabolan (*Terminalia chebula*—Tibetan *a-ru*)—the fruits are in great demand as a medicine. They are also used in dyeing, possibly for their tannin content when mordanting wool for other dyestuffs, certainly as the source of a yellowish brown dye in themselves. An alum mordant is used in the dye bath.

Tea (*Camellia theifera*—Tibetan *ja-shing*)—some refugees in India use both the leaves and the roots of the tea plant for dyeing different shades of brown on carpet wool.

Mulberry (species of *Morus*—Tibetan *dar-shing*) is said to give a reddish dye. What part of the plant is used I do not know.

Poppy (species unknown—Tibetan *leb-rgan-rtsi*)—may also have been used.

A few mineral pigments are mentioned in texts as being used for dyeing wool, namely red ochre (*btsag*), vermilion (ferrous or mercuric sulphide—Tibetan *mtshal*), red lead (*li-khri*) and some copper compound (*mthing-zhun*). No information is available on their mode of use. Some form of lime was used for bleaching wool.

Most of these dyestuffs would be little used for dyeing carpet wool except on a limited and local scale. In the best carpets, those woven for sale in the main centres of Ü and Tsang provinces, only five dyes were used—indigo, madder, lac, rhubarb and walnut. Other shades were obtained by combining these dyes or by using natural or bleached yarn.

Mordants etc.

In the above-mentioned recipes, substances other than dyestuffs proper have been referred to. Some of these are mordants, whose main function is to fix the dyestuff onto the yarn, although they may also alter its colour. Various kinds of alumaceous earth seem to have been the most important mordants, followed by copper sulphate. Other substances which come into the recipes may have been included for some mordanting effect-namely myrobalan fruit, juice from the leaves of the *zhu-mkhan* plant, and a chemical which may be zinc sulphate. Ferrous sulphate, widely used as a mordant in the west, was certainly used by the Tibetans in dyeing paper and making ink, but I have come across no specific reference to its use as a mordant in dyeing cloth.

Other substances, whose action is difficult to determine, sometimes because they are composed of many different constituents, include sour and fermenting beer, milk, whey, rhubarb juice, borax and soda, and the juice of various unidentified plants. Rhubarb juice, beer and whey (containing lactic acid) probably were active as reducing agents; borax (sodium borate) and soda (sodium carbonate) as alkalis.

Most or all of these substances were obtainable in Tibet. Alums and other sulphates were collected from beside hot springs, borax and soda from surface deposits mainly in the northern half of the country. All the substances probably had their active constituents mixed with useless impurities, and it is often impossible to tell precisely what chemical reactions were involved. Nevertheless, Tibetan dyeing practice accords well in both general principles and in many details with traditional Indian, Middle Eastern and European methods.

Chapter Three
The Tools of the Trade

Tibetan Looms and Weaving

Carpet weaving is only one of a wide range of textile arts practised by the Tibetans. Both men and women knit, make cords and braids by techniques of plaiting, and produce narrow decorated straps and bands by the 'tablet weaving' system.[1] Many nomads are good at making felt. Embroidery is employed for decorating clothing and even for making religious pictures. All these methods require no loom, but in addition the Tibetans are well acquainted with true weaving on various types of loom proper, that is, weaving on frames or between beams which allow the crossing and recrossing of warp threads which are strung upon them. On these looms they weave, in different districts, a vast range of fabrics, mainly from wool but also from cotton, silk and yak-hair, indeed everything from coarse sacking to fine serges and broadcloth. The peak of achievement is reached in Bhutan, whose weavers specialise in beautifully ornamented woollen, cotton and silk fabrics.

1. See Schuette.

The looms are of at least three quite distinct kinds, two of which are used for weaving carpets on occasion, the third exclusively so. The first kind, the commonest Tibetan loom and the simplest, is the backstrap loom.[2] It was traditionally used throughout most of Tibet by both settled and nomadic people, and may still be seen in use in most parts of the Tibetan-speaking Himalayas including Bhutan. The warp threads are stretched between a warp beam, anchored at or near the ground usually many feet in front of the weaver and a breast beam, tied to a belt or backstrap running behind her waist. The weaver sits on the ground and tensions the warp by pushing against a large stone or anchored beam with her legs. On these simple looms, village women weave narrow lengths of homespun woollen cloth. or sometimes cotton, for use as blankets, clothing, sacks and so forth. A variant form of the backstrap loom which I have seen in operation in Bhutan and in some Tibetan refugee settlements in India is employed in the latter places for weaving the material for shoulder bags. The warp threads pass round a breast beam attached to the weaver's waist, and also round the upper and lower beams of an upright rectangular frame fixed to a wall. Although cloth is the usual product of the backstrap loom, it is sometimes used for making narrow strips of knotted or looped pile carpet.

2. In most Himalayan areas the backstrap loom is called the *pang-'thag* ('pangtak').

Although the backstrap loom despite its simplicity can be used to weave fine cloth of complicated patterns, the maximum width of the finished product is only about eighteen inches, and using the loom is slow and tiring for the weaver.

The second type of loom to be considered, the horizontal frame loom on four legs[3], is better from these points of view. It is built wider and incorporates a seat for the weaver, who does not have to hold the warp in tension all the time. This category of loom is familiar in the West where it has been used by handloom weavers since the middle ages. The warp threads are unrolled progressively from the warp beam onto the breast beam as weaving proceeds. Like the backstrap loom, it is used mainly for weaving cloth and less commonly for carpets. It is difficult to estimate how widespread it was in Tibet, but in the districts where it has been observed, mainly parts of the Himalayas, it seems to be rare.

3. The horizontal frame loom is called the *khri-'thag* ('thritak').

The third kind of loom is the Tibetan carpet loom *par excellence*, and seems to be used for nothing else. It is the vertical two-beamed loom[4] in essence a heavy, upright rectangular wooden frame which supports a warp beam at the top and a breast beam at the bottom, between which the warp threads are strung. The loom is propped up against a wall or other support, and the weaver, who is more likely to be a man than with the other two looms, sits on the floor or on a low stool, weaving from the bottom upwards. This loom is little used in the Himalayas or Western Tibet, but was used for the better carpets in Ü and Tsang.

4. The vertical loom is called the *'thag-cha* or *'thag-khri* ('thakcha', 'thaktri').

Each of these three kinds of Tibetan loom may be similar in form and often in detail to looms of various neighbouring lands, whence they were presumably borrowed at unknown dates by the Tibetans (see chapter 7). Since the vertical loom is by far the most important for carpet weaving, I shall describe it first.

The Vertical Loom[5]

The vertical loom now in general use among Tibetan refugees in India, Nepal, Sikkim and Bhutan varies little from one settlement to another and as far as I have been able to find out is virtually the same as that traditionally used in Tibet and still by one or two Bhotia groups in the Himalayas. The few photographs available of older Tibetan looms show no differences, and none were mentioned by informants other than a few which I shall refer to. The loom is made of two heavy upright timbers, mortised towards their upper and lower ends to take the tenons of two rather lighter crossbeams. These four main timbers are nearly always of square or rectangular section, about three to four inches thick and forming a heavy and rigid frame.

5. A variety of this loom was described by Messinesi (see Lorentz, pp. 124–130), and briefly by Weir Hardy.
Lorentz's photograph, taken by Krause, shows a woman wearing a head-dress of the Tsang type (his fig. 40).

Also towards to top and bottom of the two uprights are four mortises running from front to back, into which are inserted the tenons of four substantial wooden pegs.[6] These are commonly cut from timber of the same section as the uprights. The pegs are sometimes replaced on looms made in India by tapered wooden blocks fixed to the uprights by steel bolts. The reason for this improvement, which dates back at least twenty years, is that the pegs tend to be pulled out, and the angle at which they project tends to be distorted, by the tension of the warp threads.

6. Tibetan *phur-pa* ('phurba').

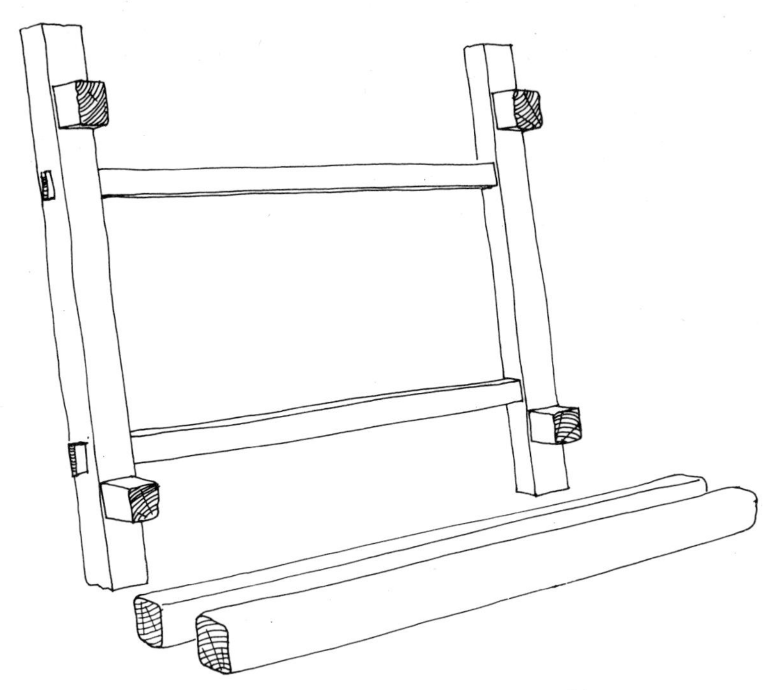

fig. 23 The traditional Tibetan vertical carpet loom.

Another way of overcoming this distortion is by wedging lengths of wood between the upper and lower pegs on each side to keep them straight, but these lengths of wood can interfere with the weaving. The mortises for the pegs must be made at least a short distance away from the mortises for the crossbeams so as not to weaken the frame unduly. The lower pegs or blocks are best located a little way below the lower crossbeam, which can then act as a fulcrum in tensioning the warp threads. The upper pegs or blocks may be placed either above or below the upper crossbeam.

Another refinement sometimes seen on recent looms, but not on older ones, is a horizontal bar about halfway up the frame. It is usually a thick bamboo pole, pushed through holes in the ends of two wooden

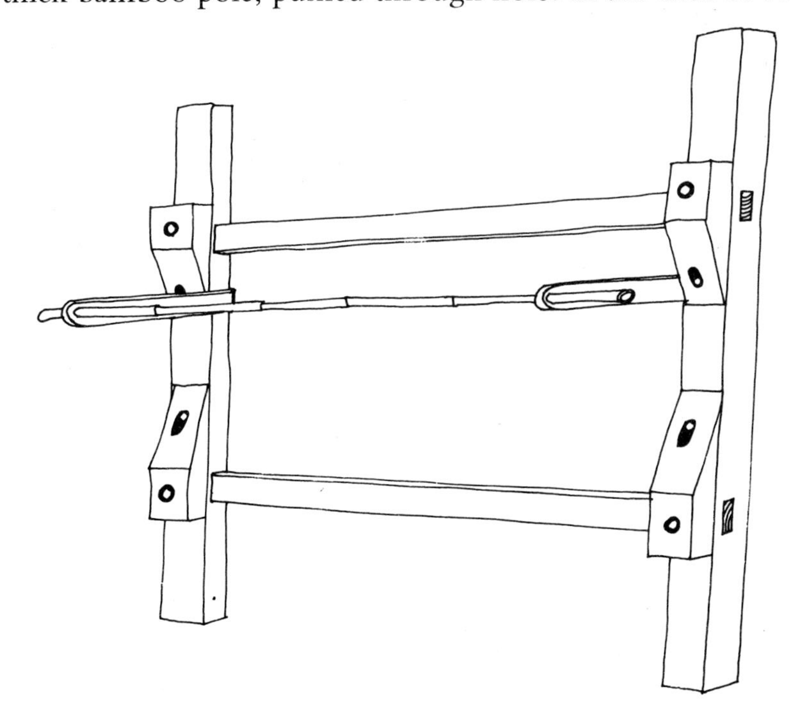

fig. 24 A modified vertical loom as used by many refugees. The pegs are replaced by bolted-on blocks and there is a bamboo 'heddle-pole'.

arms which are nailed or screwed to the uprights, holding the bar about eighteen inches out in front of the loom, that is, towards the weaver. The pole is used as an aid in manipulating the heddle rod and is said to have been copied from Indian looms since the arrival of the refugees.

The breast beam and warp beam, around which the warp threads will be wound, are not part of the structure of the frame. The warp beam rests on the top pair of pegs or blocks, while the breast beam is held up against the bottom surface of the lower pegs by the tension of the warp threads. The two beams do not revolve. They are made of timber of a section at least as heavy as the uprights of the frame, preferably about three to four inches thick and up to six inches deep in order to resist bending, and they should be at least two inches longer than the width of the main frame, so that they project slightly on either side of the loom. Their edges are rounded and smoothed to allow the warp threads to slide easily round them.

The standard size of the loom is about five feet square, though variation is possible. The standard size gives ample room to weave a carpet of about three feet by six, which is the usual size of carpet now woven in India and Nepal and rather larger than most carpets woven

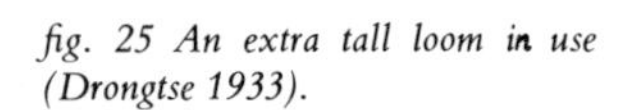

fig. 25 An extra tall loom in use (Drongtse 1933).

in Tibet. The exceptions were long carpets intended to cover corridor floors or temple pillars, Sir Charles Bell photographed a loom of standard width but at least fifteen feet high, provided with several sets of upper peg mortises to enable carpets of various lengths to be woven, up to about thirty feet. Because of a demand for rugs of twelve feet by nine among American buyers in recent years, several refugee settlements have installed looms about ten feet high by fifteen feet wide. These all have the bar for working the heddle rod, which would otherwise be too heavy to manage. At least one refugee enterprise has a loom with rollers instead of stationary beams, as used by some Persian and Indian carpet weavers. On it, very long carpets about ten feet wide are woven using the traditional Tibetan knotting system, chiefly for the floors of Indian cinema halls.

The basic loom, like some other Tibetan constructions such as buildings, is easily and cheaply made, relying for its strength mainly on its weight; a simple but workmanlike piece of apparatus. When well made from a hard, strong wood it is long lasting, although if the timbers are weak or the jointing poor, the powerful tension of the warp threads will soon distort the frame. Bent breast beams and warp beams are often to be seen, though a clever weaver can compensate for

fig. 26 Extra large loom in the refugee settlement at Paonta Sahib, Himachal Pradesh, 1972.

this and other distortions by inserting wedges and packing at various points. The loom takes up little space leaning against a wall, and is often set up in a verandah to take advantage of the light and shelter available there. It is easily dismantled, and because the method of stringing allows a half-finished carpet to be taken off a loom and put back on it, the whole apparatus can be taken to pieces for storage or transport at any stage. Unfortunately the loom is heavy, which is no doubt one reason why it is not used by nomads. It would not be difficult to design an improved loom using less wood and at the same time more resistant to distortion and lighter to transport, all of which advantages would have been useful in Tibet. Nevertheless the traditional loom serves its purpose well enough, and has enabled the weavers to develop their skills to remarkable heights.

Other Tools

A number of pieces of accessory equipment are needed to weave a carpet. Their exact functions will become clear during the description of the weaving process, but for convenience I shall list them here.

When the loom is strung the continuous warp is wound round a horizontal rod as well as round the breast beam and warp beam. It is known as a 'hrok' (Tsang dialect) which I translate as 'axis-rod'.[7] It used to be made of hard wood, but is now usually a metal rod or tube of a quarter to half an inch in diameter, since the more rigid it is the better.

7. Tibetan *srog*. Presumably it would be pronounced 'sok' in the Lhasa dialect. This is the Tibetan word for 'life', also used for the axis of various things such as the centre pole of a Buddhist reliquary or *mchod-rten*, and for an axle-rod (both called *srog-shing*). Several Tibetans have explained to me that the axis-rod is the most important part of the whole loom, since if it is withdrawn (before any weaving is begun) the whole warp or basis of the carpet disintegrates, just as does the body of any creature whose life is taken away.

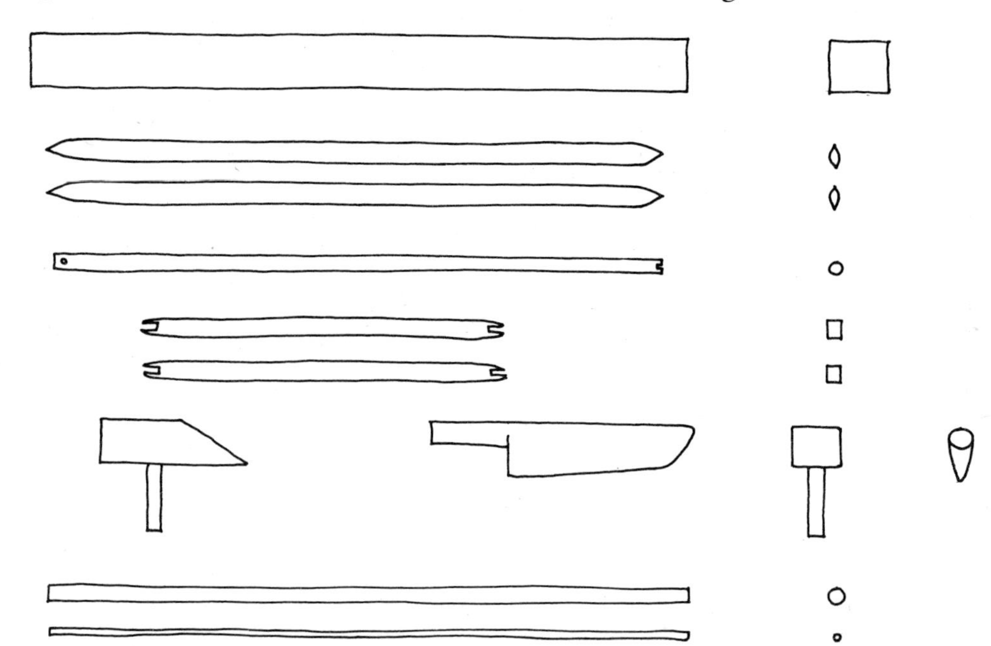

fig. 27 Tools and accessories for the vertical loom. From top to bottom: lever, shed sticks, heddle rod, spools, mallet and beater-in ('tak'), axis-rod, gauge-rod.

The odd and even threads of the warp at the front of the loom are separated from one another by two shed sticks, enabling a shed and a countershed to be held between the two sets of threads. They are identical in shape and size, a little longer than the width of the carpet to be woven, about two inches wide and a quarter of an inch thick, with pointed ends for easy movement between the warp threads. They must be made of strong wood. The job of the upper stick is to separate the warp threads of the odd and even sets by a space known as the countershed through which the weft can be thrown. At the same time it restrains all the warp threads by friction from moving sideways and becoming tangled together or crossed—thus it also acts as a 'lease rod' in western terms. Once inserted into the countershed it is not moved in the course of weaving except to be turned on its long axis to alter the width of the countershed. After the relative positions of the two sets of warp threads below this upper shed stick have been reversed by pulling the far, even set towards the weaver, the new 'shed' so formed is maintained by inserting the lower shed stick into it. When the countershed again required, the lower shed stick is simply pulled out of the shed sideways, and the even threads spring back of their own accord. On old Tibetan looms the shed sticks were often just thin bamboos. Although the two have slightly different functions, they are given the same name in Tibetan; 'wolu' or 'wulu'.[8]

8. I am not sure of the spelling of this word. A syllable *'ur* is said to mean 'between' in some southern dialects—possibly related to *dbar*, 'between' in colloquial Lhasa Tibetan. The second syllable is probably *blugs* 'put in'—thus the whole word may mean 'put in between', i.e. between the odd and even sets of threads.

Crossing the warp threads, that is pulling the even set forwards, is achieved with the aid of a heddle rod attached by 'leashes' of cord to each warp thread of the odd set. It is simply a wooden rod about the same length as the shed sticks and about an inch in diameter, called a 'nenyu'.[9] The name suggests that it was originally made of bamboo. Traditionally it has a hole bored through it at one end and a groove cut across the face of the other end. If the loom is provided with a projecting bar as already described, the heddle rod is linked to this at each end by a harness consisting of two cords of unequal length attached to the ends of a short stick which straddles the bar. When the warp is under tension, the heddle rod can be held close to the warp or farther from it by manipulating the harnesses so that either the longer or the shorter cords take the strain. With this arrangement the lower shed stick is redundant, since the shed is held open by tension through the shorter cords of the harnesses.

9. Either *snal-smyug* or *snad-smyug*. *snal-ma* is given in dictionaries for 'warp-yarn'. But the first syllable when pronounced alone in the Tsang dialect ends with a glottal stop, suggesting a *-d* final. Benedict has reconstructed an original Tibeto-Burman word **s-nat* meaning 'heddle' from various cognates in Burmese and other languages (Benedict, p. 106).

Weft threads are thrown across through the shed and countershed on a pair of spool-type shuttles[10] which are simply sticks up to a foot long. The weft yarn may be wound on the spool from end to end between a pair of notches, or round its thickness. Some weavers use only one spool, others use none at all but just push a ball of yarn through the shed and countershed by hand.

10. The word for 'shuttle' is pronounced something like 'phushing'.

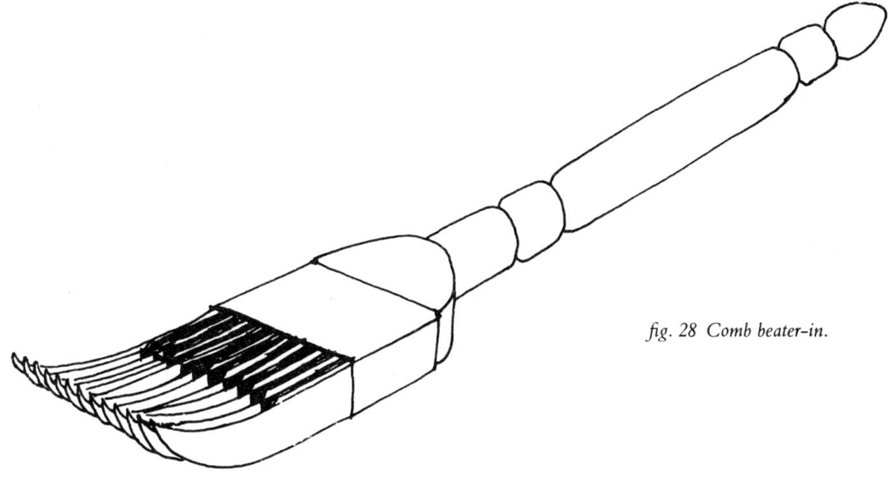

fig. 28 Comb beater-in.

After the wefts have been thrown, they must be pressed firmly down with the end of a 'beater-in', Tibetan 'tak'.[11] This tool is essentially a wooden handle which merges into a blade. The end of the blade is at an angle of about 70 degrees to the handle. There are at least two distinct designs of beater-in. One resembles a meat chopper with a straight blade, except that it is the shorter edge of the blade which makes contact with the work. The other has a blade which continues the line of the handle in a curve. The tool is usually carved out of a single block of wood. It has now been largely replaced in India by a toothed beater-in or comb beater, copied from Indian models and similar to types used in the Middle East. A row of curving metal teeth are set into a solid wooden head, to which is attached a straight handle, the whole tool being about a foot long.

11. I can find no spelling for this word. Desgodins had *stag-so*, '*Instrumentum textoris, radius*, navette du tisserand'.

After each weft or pair of wefts has been beaten in, the pile is knotted or looped by winding the pile yarn around both the warp threads

12. The first syllable of this word is presumably *rgyug* as in *rgyug-pa* 'stick'.

and a thin gauge-rod which is gradually moved across as knotting proceeds. The gauge-rod or 'gyukshu'[12] used to be made of wood with a single groove running along its whole length. Nowadays a metal rod of up to a quarter of an inch in diameter is preferred. After each row of knotting, the gauge-rod and its knots must be beaten down hard against the previous rows with a mallet (Tibetan 'thowa', the ordinary word for mallet or hammer). Its head is heavy but tapers at one end to a narrow edge. The size of this mallet varies up to a maximum of about a nine-inch long head on a foot-long handle. The final stages of the knotting cycle are the cutting of the knots along the rod with a small sharp knife, and roughly trimming the pile with a pair of scissors. When the whole carpet has been knotted, another small pair of scissors is used for vertical cutting between adjacent colours of the design, and a large flat pair for fine shearing of the surface.

Other items of equipment required are a piece of timber at least two feet long for use as a lever in tensioning the warp; some rope for lashing the breast beam and warp beam to the frame; and scraps of wood for use as wedges and packing. Further tools which may be used in tentering and teaseling the finished carpet will be briefly described later.

Most of the ancillary equipment of carpet weaving, like the loom itself, is simple in design and made of wood. The only essential metal tools are the knife and scissors. No nails or glue were traditionally used in constructing the loom. In India and Nepal, metal components such as screws, bolts, nails and rods are readily available at fairly low prices and have crept into the weaver's equipment; also a few details such as the heddle bar and the comb beater have been copied from Indian looms. Otherwise the vertical loom and its mode of operation have remained faithful to the traditional patterns.

The Horizontal Frame Loom

This type of loom is rather more complicated than the vertical loom, but still simple compared with most European handlooms. I have seen photographs of four different examples, all of a standard design and all from different parts of the Himalayas and of two examples from Tibet proper. The design may vary in other areas of Tibet. In some places this loom is looked on with disfavour because the weaver sits on a raised seat, a privilege often reserved for lamas and others of high status.

Like the vertical loom, it is made of wood. The main frame consists of two side beams, running fore and aft, joined about a third of the way from one end by a crossbeam tenoned through them. Four sloping legs, also tenoned through the side beams and projecting some six or nine inches above them, hold the frame about two feet from the ground. An upright projects from each side beam about half way along its length, bearing a short bar on top, parallel to the side beam. A bamboo pole rests across these bars above the frame, prevented from slipping off by raised stops on the ends of the bars. It serves as an axle for two wooden pulleys. Cords slung over these pulleys connect two heddle frames to one another in such a way that raising one frame automatically

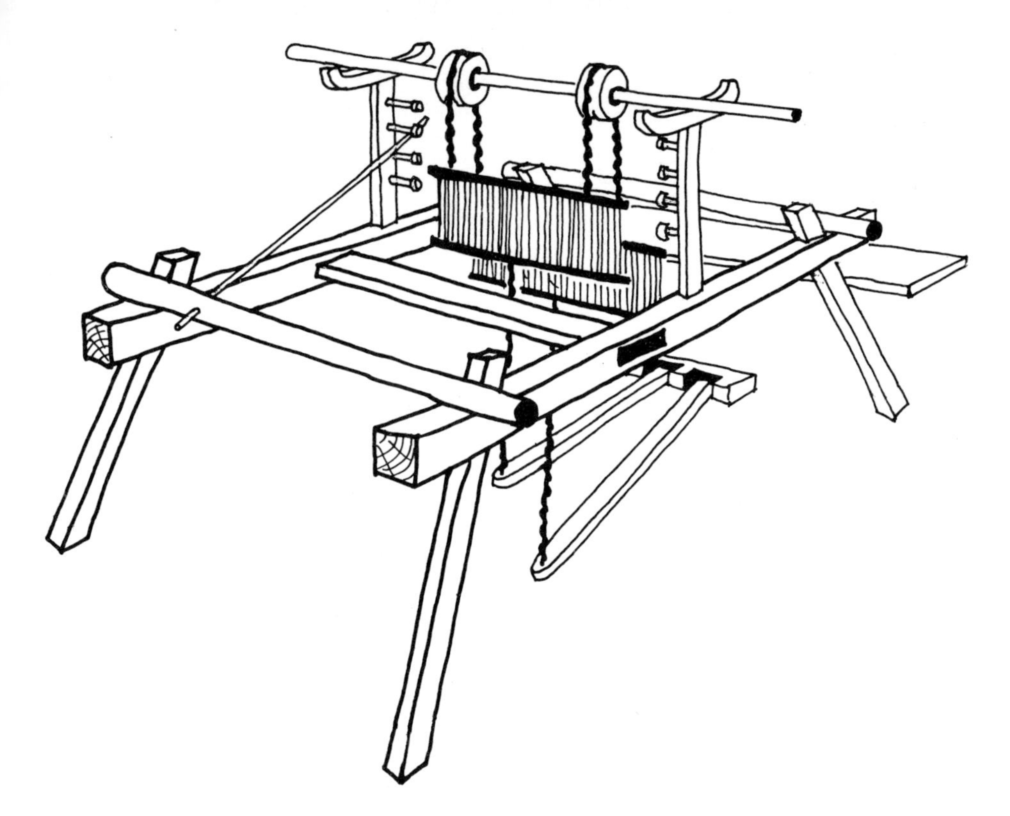

fig. 29 The traditional Tibetan horizontal frame loom.

fig. 30 A Sherpa woman weaving cloth on a horizontal frame loom.

lowers the other. Each heddle frame consists of two rods running across the loom and conected by the necessary number of leashes, cords about a foot long. Raising and lowering of the frames is done via cords leading down to two foot pedals which are simply lengths of wood resting on the ground at the end nearer the weaver. A plank for the weaver to sit on is fixed across the legs at the end opposite the crossbeam.

The warp beam and breast beam take the form of wooden rollers, held by the tension of the warps in large notches cut into the projecting upper ends of the legs. Each beam is split lengthways into two parts, between which the warp threads are gripped with the aid of cloth bindings. Before being so gripped, the warp threads are tied at each end to a pole or 'heading rod' which lies alongside its beam and revolves with it, preventing the ends of the threads from slipping through between the two parts of the beam. As weaving proceeds the warp threads are rolled from breast beam to warp beam. To prevent these beams from revolving while under tension, one end of a rod is inserted into a hole bored through each beam, and its other end restrained against a peg in one of the uprights, or against the crossbeam of the frame.

Shed sticks are not required, since the shed and countershed are made by the movement of the two heddle frames, one of which is connected to the odd threads, the other to the even. The functions of laze rod and beater-in are combined in a reed. This is a comb-like device, slightly wider than the width of the cloth to be woven. Pieces of split bamboo about six to nine inches long are held at their ends in grooves cut along the top and bottom bars, which are held in position by two end pieces let into notches at the bar ends. One warp thread is led through each space or 'dent' between each bamboo tooth and its neighbour, and thus cannot tangle with other warp threads. By pulling the reed sharply towards her, the weaver can beat in the wefts with its teeth. One or more weft spools, a gauge-rod and a knife are required for weaving carpets on the horizontal loom, as for the vertical loom.

The Backstrap Loom[13]

The backstrap loom is traditionally used almost exclusively by women. It has no frame as such—merely wooden crosspieces of various kinds, held in place on the warp threads by the tension exerted by the weaver's legs. Despite the dissimilar appearance, the weaving system is identical in principle to that of the vertical loom, and quite different from that of the horizontal frame loom, in that a continuous warp is looped alternately forwards and backwards round an 'axis rod', and passes round a non-revolving breast beam and warp beam.

The number of crosspieces used depends on the type of cloth being woven. The backstrap, usually of fabric, is attached to the breast beam and provided with two short sticks at the ends to keep it flat. The breast beam is usually split lengthwise into two parts between which the web is gripped, the two parts being bound with cloth. It is necessary to grip the web to prevent it being pushed round the breast beam when beating in. The warp beam is a single piece of wood, tied to a tree or fixed somehow to the ground. The beater-in is not like that of the vertical loom, but is a heavy bar the width of the web, with rounded edges and tapering down to the edge nearest the weaver. Into this edge a metal blade is set. Heddle rod, shed sticks and axis-rod are the same as

13. M. Corneille Jest has filmed this loom in use in Dolpo, northwest Nepal. It was observed by Moorcroft in the early 19th century (see Moorcroft & Trebeck, vol. II, pp. 72–74). See also Ephraim.

fig. 31 A backstrap loom in use, Dolpo, northwest Nepal.

for the vertical loom. In addition a laze rod is used which is simply a stick around which the warp threads are twisted to keep them apart. A wide plank resting against heavy stones on the ground provides a fixed point against which the weaver pushes with her feet. This is all the equipment needed for weaving a carpet on the backstrap loom, together with the usual spools, gauge-rod and knife. If the fabric base of the carpet is to be given a twill weave, two more heddles stick will be required.

Chapter Four
Making a Carpet

Before weaving can begin, the loom must be 'dressed' or fitted up with warp threads, heddles, shed sticks and so forth. This can be a lengthy process taking several days for the bigger looms.

Dressing the Vertical Loom[1]

1. The process of making a carpet on the vertical loom has been briefly described by Messinesi and Weir Hardy.

Unlike the horizontal looms, whose warps are first laid onto sticks and then transferred to the loom itself, the vertical loom is 'mounted' or strung with the warp direct. Although if space is restricted or if the loom is very large this may be done with the loom upright, mounting the warp is easier with the loom frame flat on its back on the floor. The breast beam and warp beam are laid in position across the uprights outside the pegs. It may be necessary to place some wooden packing between the breast beam and its pegs to leave a gap between the breast beam and the lower crossbeam of the frame which is just wide enough to take the end of the tensioning lever. The warp beam and breast beam are then lashed to the frame upright with rope, not too tightly but with secure knots so that they cannot spring away from the frame when under tension.

fig. 32 The system of mounting the warp of the vertical loom.

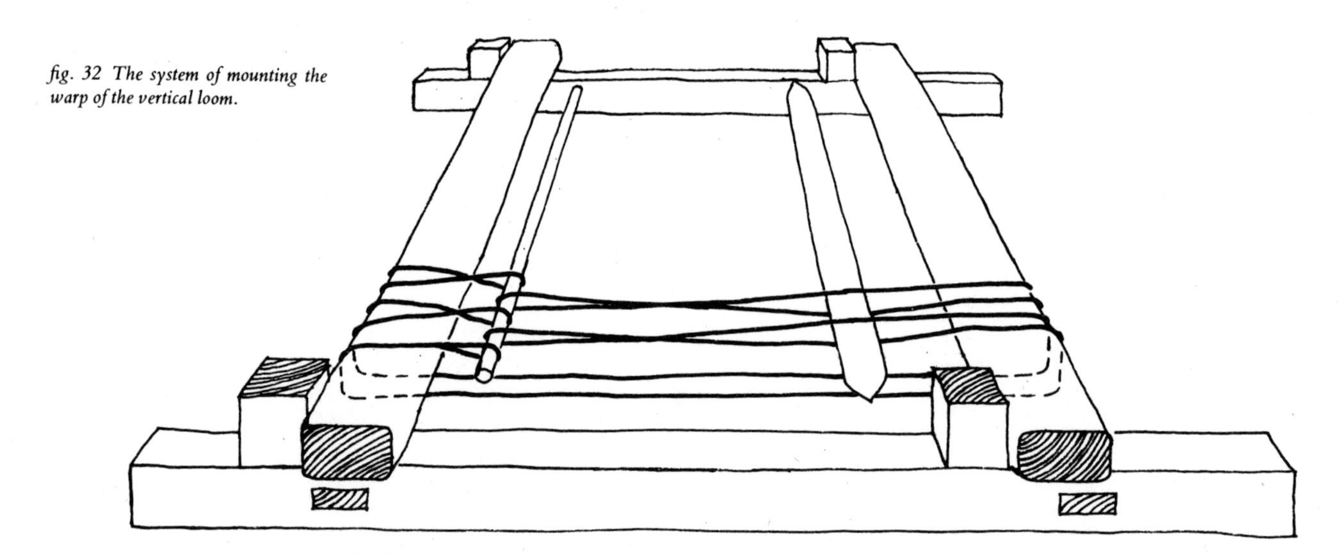

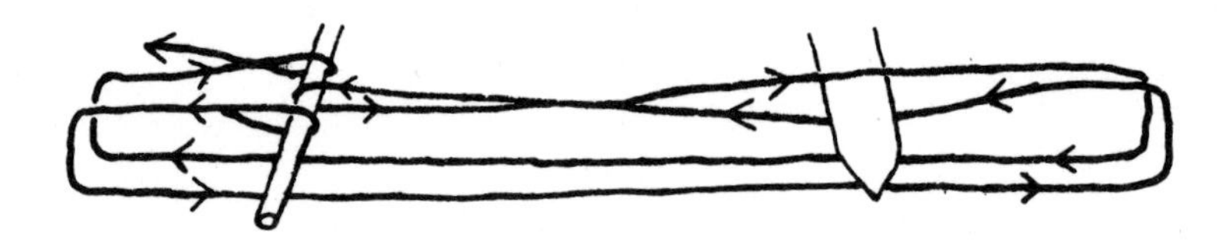

With the warp yarn ready to hand and rolled into balls, the axis-rod is laid across the frame about a foot from the breast beam, and the upper shed stick is also laid across about the same distance from the warp beam. A loop tied in the end of the warp yarn is slipped over the axis-rod near its right hand end, as it will be when the carpet is being woven. The mounting of the warp yarn now proceeds. In one complete mounting cycle, the yarn is led over and under the breast beam, under and over the warp beam, under the shed stick, round the axis-rod and back over the shed stick, over and under the warp beam, under and over the breast beam and back to the axis-rod again. One mounting cycle follows another continuously. The principle is that every time the yarn meets either of the two beams or the axis-rod in its gradual leftward progress across the loom, it makes a U-turn round it and returns in the direction from which it came. It always turns round the axis-rod from above, that is, from the side which will eventually face the weaver. Each ball of warp yarn is joined to the next when it runs out. Thus all the warp threads manipulated while weaving at the front of the loom are really only parts of a single continuous warp thread, which is prevented from unravelling by the axis-rod.

When the required number of warp threads, or, strictly, the required number of turns of the single warp thread have been mounted, the end

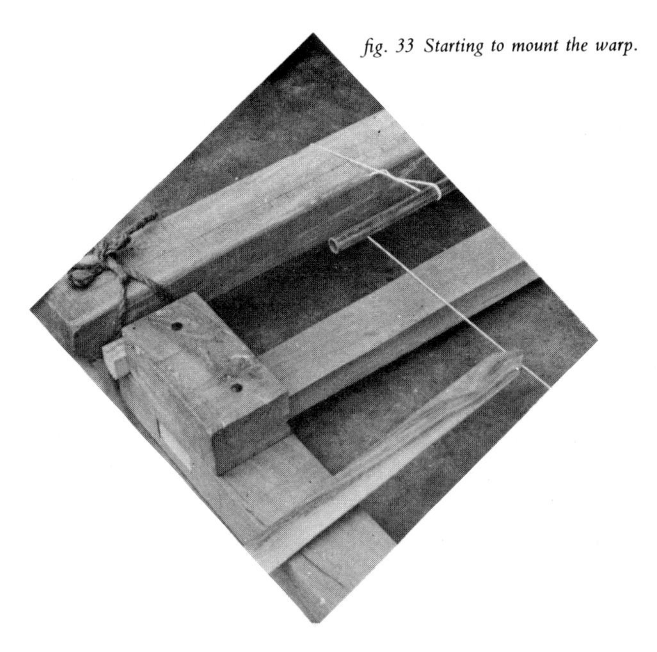

fig. 33 Starting to mount the warp.

of the yarn is tied into a loop which is slipped over the left hand end of the axis-rod, ideally at the end of a complete mounting cycle as already described. If this is done halfway through a cycle, that is, on a thread leading from the warp beam, there will be an odd number of threads at the front of the loom, when counted either on one side of the axis-rod or the other. This does not greatly matter, as one thread may be left off the carpet at one edge, or the discrepancy can be disguised by the carpet's edge binding. Traditionally there is always an odd number of pairs of threads (making an even number of total threads) on each side of the axis-rod. As the normal carpet knot is made on two threads, there must be a thread left over if the total number of single warp

fig. 34 Mounting the warp in progress on an extra large loom, Paonta Sahib. The axis rod is suspended against the breast beam.

threads is odd. The middle pair of threads, one odd and one even, is often marked with coloured ink or powder as an aid in composing the pattern of the pile.[2]

2. The middle pair of threads are known as the *dkyil-thag*.

The loom is then leant in nearly vertical position against a wall. The weight of the breast beam as it falls will stretch the warp threads somewhat, and these are then spaced evenly across the intended width of the carpet along the breast beam. At the warp beam they are also evenly spaced, but splayed slightly to give about two inches of extra width. This is to compensate for the drawing in of the carpet edges by the wefts as weaving goes ahead.

fig. 35 Tensioning the loom with the lever after the warp has been mounted.

The next stage is tensioning, done at each side of the loom in turn by inserting the end of a wooden lever into the gap between the breast beam and the lower crossbeam of the frame, and forcing the breast beam down while inserting packing between it and the lower pegs. Judging the correct tension is a matter of experience and varies a good deal from one weaver to another. With a lever of the size mentioned, tensioning usually requires the efforts of two people; one leaning against the loom and inserting packing, the other pressing down hard on the lever. It can be a risky operation, as the force applied can crack a weak loom or cause the lever to jump out and injure the operators. The bigger looms need very long levers, pressed down by the weight of several people sitting on them. It is important that the tension should be even right across the loom. If the frame is distorted, extra packing may be needed above one end of the breast beam, or even between some of the threads and the warp beam, but if the frame is true and if the beams and the axis-rod are smooth enough, the warp threads should automatically slide over them to stretch evenly as the loom is being tensioned. This is a significant advantage conferred by the use of the axis-rod system.

The warp threads at the front of the loom (facing the weaver) have now been divided above the axis-rod, and because they loop over it, into an odd set slightly towards the back and an even set slightly towards the front, counting from the left, with a shed or space between the two sets. Somewhere between the axis-rod and the upper shed stick, the two sets cross along a line or 'lease', and reverse positions. Above the lease, the upper shed stick forms and occupies the countershed between the odd set of threads to the front and the even set to the back. The lower shed stick is now inserted into the shed between the axis-rod and the lease, and it is twisted to the horizontal in order to open the shed

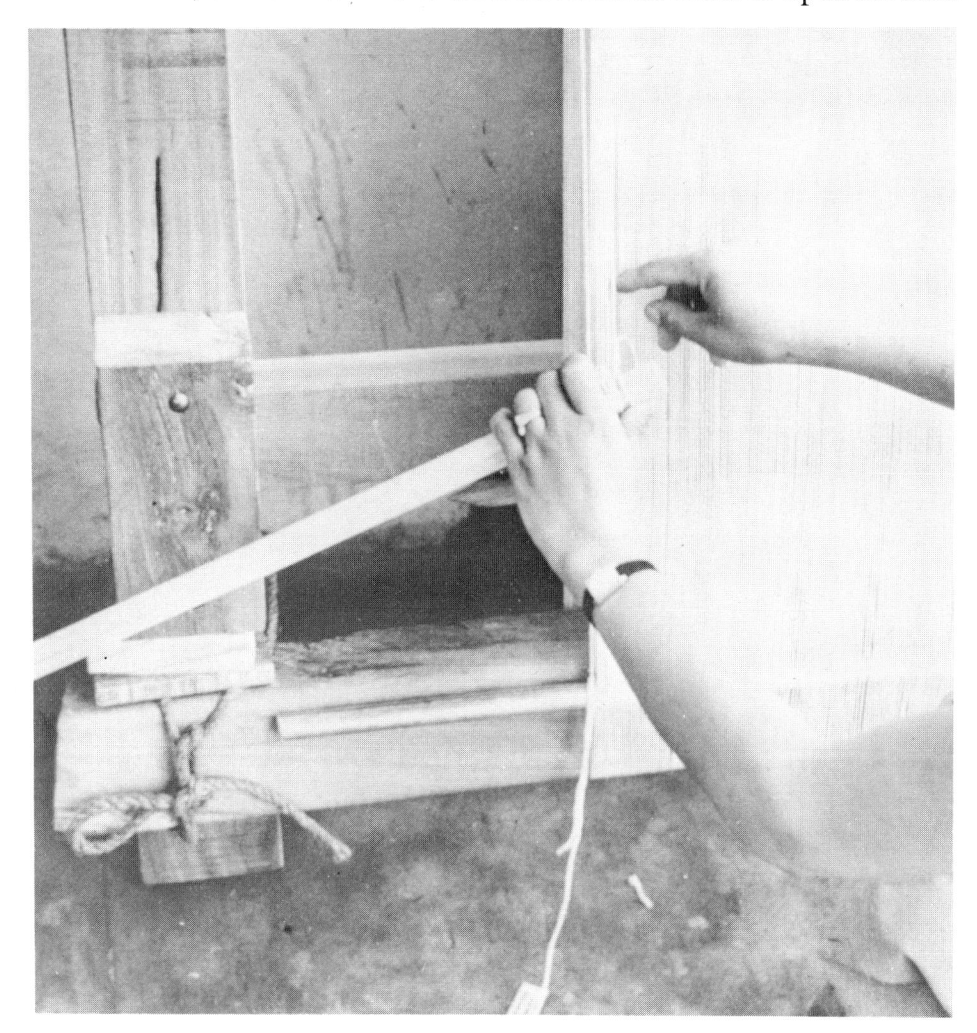

fig. 36 Stringing the heddle rod.

wider. The heddle rod is now strung onto the threads of the even set, to the front below the lease, by means of 'leashes' of cord. There are two ways of doing this. The first way is to tie a loop in the end of a ball of cord and to push this loop from right to left through the shed so that the cord occupies the position of a weft thread. The loop is slipped over the right hand end of the heddle rod which is held in the left hand at the left side of the loom. Then beginning from the left, a loop of this 'weft' cord is pulled through between each even warp thread and its neighbour with the right hand, and the heddle rod is pushed progressively through these loops or leashes as they are made, up to the right hand edge. When this is finished, the right hand end of the cord is tied into a loop which is slipped round the right hand end of the heddle rod, the original loop by now having reached the other end. The leashes are held loosely in place by tying another length of cord through the hole bored in one end of the heddle rod, leading it over the leashes, across the groove at the other end, and tying it round that end of the heddle rod. In the second method of stringing, the leashes are knotted together along the rod, making them more secure. The rod is prepared by stretching along it a holding cord which consists of four or five strands of cord twisted together and tied to the rod at each end. The rod is then hung in front of the warp threads and stringing begins from the right. One end of the leash cord is tied to holding cord, and then pushed in a ball between the first two even warp threads above the heddle rod, behind the first of these, back under the heddle rod, under itself from the left, once round the holding cord from above, and back between the second and third even warp threads, and so on.

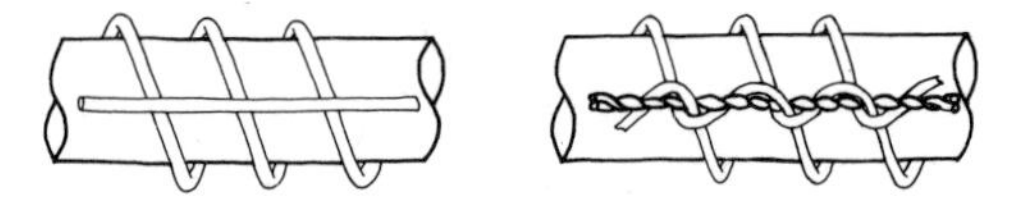

fig. 37 Two alternative ways of arranging the leashes along the heddle rod.

After stringing the heddle rod, the lower shed stick is twisted to the vertical, and the loom is now ready for work to begin. For the purposes of description I shall divide the work of making the carpet's fabric base and its pile into two types; weaving and knotting, made up of successive repetitions of the Weaving Cycle and the Knotting Cycle respectively. Before either can begin, the end binding must be twisted in and the edge binding started.

Edge and End Binding

From now on, the loom is kept propped up against a wall or other support and the weaver sits on the floor or on a low stool. There are five essential parts to a finished carpet: the warp threads, the end binding, the edge binding, the weft threads[3] and the pile. The warp threads have already been dealt with. The end binding yarn is tied to the extreme left hand pair of warp threads (one odd and one even) about two inches above the axis-rod, pinching these two threads together. It is led behind the next pair, round in front of them and behind again below itself, and so on to the right edge. The end of a ball of edge binding yarn is then tied onto each end pair of warp threads, immediately above the end

3. The word for a 'weft thread' is *khog-spun*; *khog* being the space between the two sets of warp threads—that is, the shed or countershed.

fig. 38 One row of end binding is completed, the edge binding has been wound in, and a second row of end binding is in progress.

binding, which is then led back from right to left immediately above the previous line, so that the loops of the two rows of end binding interlock in herringbone fashion. The end binding yarn is tied again to the left hand pair of warp threads, and any surplus is cut off. The two balls of edge binding, one at each side, are then wound first round the two outermost pairs of warp threads, and then again round the two outermost groups of three. This winding in of the edge binding is repeated between every two wefts along the whole carpet.

The Weaving Cycle

The next stage is to produce a narrow strip of plain weave with about four to six wefts, to act as a firm base against which to beat the first few rows of pile knots. This involves several operations of the weaving cycle, half of which is also performed after every row of pile knots along the carpet. For this end weaving, the type of yarn which will later be used in knotting the pile is often employed.

The Weaving Cycle is made up of the following stages: 1. opening the shed. 2. throwing the weft through the shed. 3. beating the weft. 4. producing the countershed. 5. winding in the edge binding. 6. opening the countershed. 7. throwing the weft through the countershed. 8. beating the weft. 9. producing the shed. 10. winding in the edge binding.

Having opened the shed by twisting the lower shed stick to the horizontal, the weft yarn which is wound on a single spool, is thrown across through the shed. The lower shed stick is then twisted to the vertical and brought down lightly on the weft to beat it down. It is then withdrawn from the shed sideways, automatically opening the countershed as the even warp threads jump to the back. If the heddle rod is provided with a bar and harnesses. this crossing of the warp threads to produce the countershed is achieved by letting the harnesses slide towards the loom. The lower shed stick is then replaced in the countershed and pulled down to make sure all the warp threads have crossed and to bring the lease or crossing-line right down to the weft.

The edge binding is wound in as before; round two and then three warp threads at each side. The countershed is opened wider by twisting the lower shed stick to the horizontal, or, if preferred, by twisting the upper shed stick, the lower one having been withdrawn first. The weft yarn is then thrown back through the countershed on its spool. The even warp threads must now be brought to the front to produce the shed again. This is easy if a heddle bar and harnesses are provided—the harnesses are pulled back and automatically hold the heddle rod in the correct position. Without these aids, the operation is slower and more difficult. Having withdrawn the lower shed stick from the countershed, the weaver grasps the heddle rod firmly with the thumb (uppermost) and forefinger of her left hand at the rod's right hand end (or vice versa), pulling the heddle rod towards her and at the same time pushing away both odd and even warp threads just below the heddle rod with her other fingers, while inserting the tip of the lower shed stick into the newly formed shed with her other hand. This awkward manoeuvre must be repeated several times across the width of the carpet until the lower shed stick has been pushed all the way through. It is then pulled down to move the lease down to just above the previous weft. Finally, the edge binding is wound in again to complete one Weaving Cycle.

fig. 39 The vertical loom with the warp mounted and tensioned, the heddle rod strung, the shed sticks in place and the end binding and end weaving completed. The two balls of dark yarn are the edge binding.

The Knotting Cycle[4]

The Knotting Cycle is made up of; a) tying a row of knots. b) pulling them tight and beating them down. c) making half a weaving cycle, either stages 1 to 4 or 6 to 9. d) beating-in. e) cutting and trimming the knots. f) winding in the edge binding.

4. The word for 'knot' is *mdud-pa*.

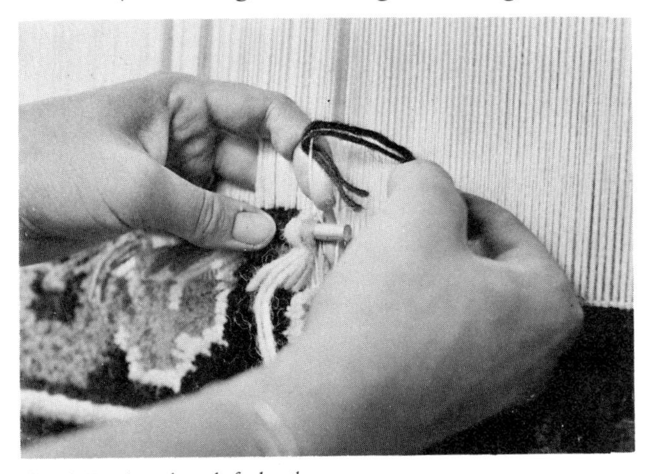

fig. 40 Knotting: the end of a length of yarn of a new colour is slipped round a warp thread.

fig. 41 Knotting: the end of the yarn has been moved down until it projects below the gauge-rod.

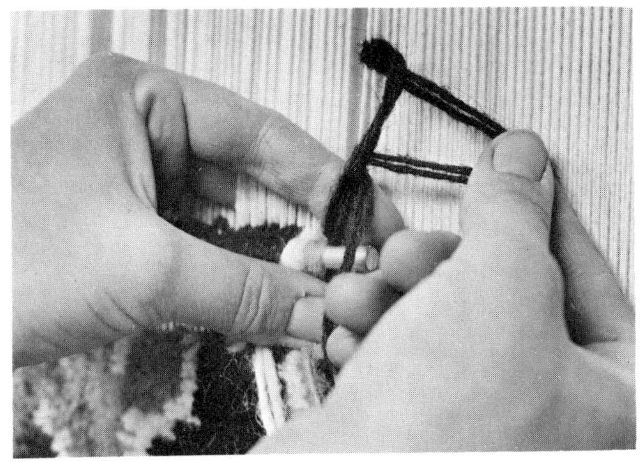

fig. 42 Knotting: the continuation of the yarn has been passed behind and round the second warp thread.

fig. 43 Knotting: the loop has been slipped over the end of the gauge-rod.

fig. 44 Knotting: the loop is being pulled tight round the gauge-rod.

fig. 45 The gauge-rod with its knots. The yarn of the right-hand colour has been left above the rod; that of the other colours, below.

After the desired amount of plain weave has been completed, the first row of knots is tied across the carpet from left to right, with the aid of the gauge-rod. When beginning a line (and when starting a new colour within a line) a special sort of knot is usually tied. The loose end of a ball of the pile yarn is taken from left to right behind the third warp thread from the left hand edge, then pulled forwards to the right of it either above or below the gauge-rod, which is hung or held to the left, its right hand end level with the knot being tied. The continuation of the yarn towards the ball is then taken to the right in front of the third and fourth warp threads, and pushed back leftwards behind the fourth thread in a loop which is pulled forwards between the two warp threads (below itself) and slipped over the end of the gauge-rod. (All references to left and right are from the point of view of the weaver.) The continuation of the yarn can then be pulled lightly so that the knot grips the threads and the rod.

For the next knot, and all subsequent knots of the same colour, the continuation of the yarn is led up behind the gauge-rod, rightwards in front of the next rightward pair of warp threads (the first of which should be odd, the second even), then leftwards behind them both and forwards (below itself) to the left of both of them in a loop as before. The gauge-rod is pushed progressively towards the right as the loops are slipped over it. The last knot of a particular colour of yarn may be finished by leaving the continuation of the yarn either above or below the gauge-rod, and likewise the first knot of a subsequent colour may be started with the projecting end either above or below the rod. These and other refinements of knotting will be discussed later.

All Tibetan weavers I have seen tie the knots successively from left to right, changing colour as and when demanded by the pattern. I have never observed the practice, sometimes found in the Middle East, of tying all the knots of each colour in turn. When two weavers work on the same carpet, one will start from the left hand edge, the other from the centre, both working from left to right each with her own gauge-rod.

fig. 46 Diagram showing how the pile yarn is wound in relation to the warp and weft threads, before being cut. The central part of the gauge-rod is shown in dotted lines for the sake of clarity. The far left-hand knot is the first one of a colour.

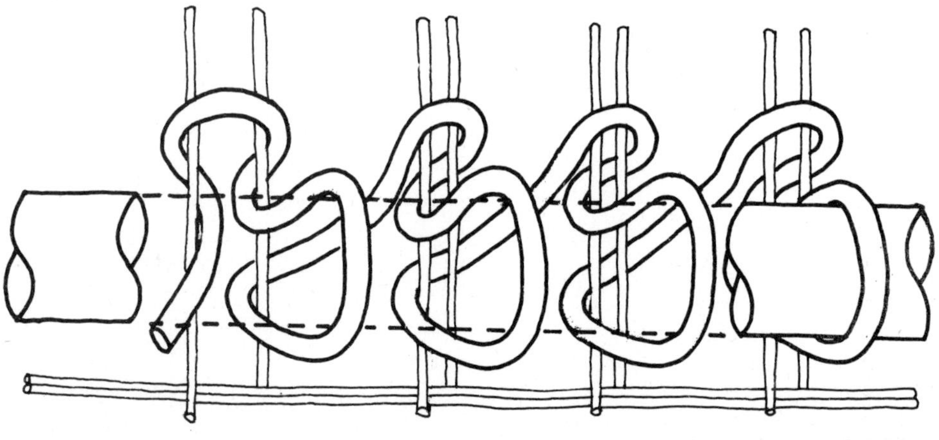

When a row of knotting is finished, any yarn still joined to its ball is cut off, and the hanging ends of pile yarn are pulled to tighten the grip of the knots round the warp threads and the rod. Then the gauge-rod with all its knots is beaten firmly down against the previous weft thread with the sharp edge of the mallet, the weaver's free hand continuing to tighten the knots as they descend. It is claimed that beating will be more even if the right hand half of the rod is beaten using the mallet in the right hand, and the left hand half using it in the left.

Half a weaving cycle must now be made. If the warp threads leave a shed between them, then stages 1 to 4 will be performed; if a countershed, then stages 6 to 9. The wefts thrown between rows of pile knots differ from those thrown in the plain weave at the ends of the carpet in that they are of a different material (cotton yarn, the same as the warp threads or special woollen weft yarn) and in that they are double instead of single. The usual method is to throw two spools across in opposite directions, although some weavers throw a single spool first one way and then the other. In either case, the warp threads are crossed not between the two weft throws, but only after both have been made.

Next, the reinserted lower shed stick is twisted to the horizontal, opening the shed or countershed wider, and the weft threads are beaten-in hard with the beater-in ('tak') or comb beater. If the 'tak' is used, it is gripped like a dagger poised for a downward blow in the hand which is pushed through the front set of warp threads at some point across the web into the shed or countershed. The short or curved edge of the blade is rammed down onto the lease where the two sets of warp threads cross immediately over the weft threads. The wefts are actually pushed down by these warp threads. If the comb beater is used, its teeth, curving either upwards or downwards, are simply pushed between the warp threads from the front, and brought down sharply directly onto the weft threads. In either case the operation is repeated right across the carpet. The lower shed stick is then twisted to the vertical position.

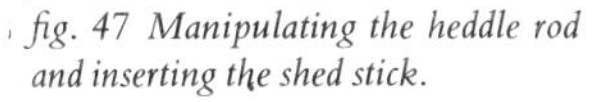

fig. 47 Manipulating the heddle rod and inserting the shed stick.

fig. 48 Throwing the spool.

fig. 49 Beating-in with the 'tak'.

fig. 50 Cutting the knots along the gauge-rod with a chisel.

fig. 51 Trimming the cut knots with a pair of scissors.

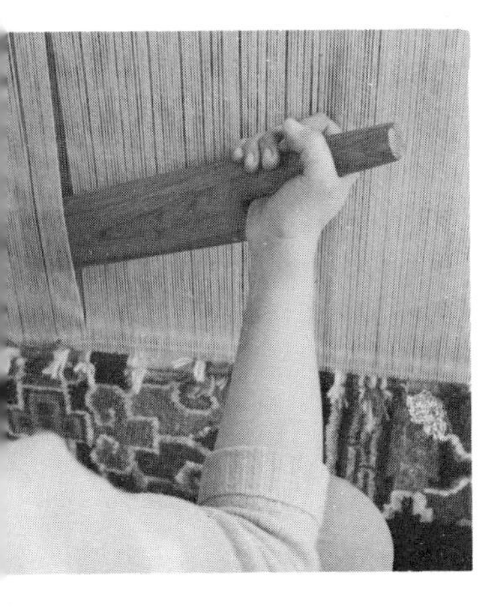

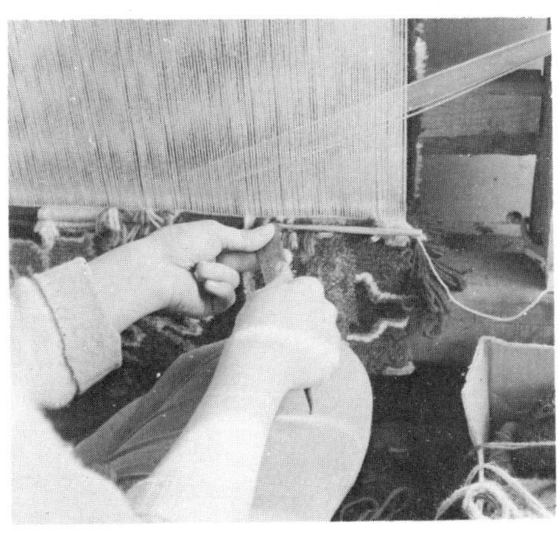

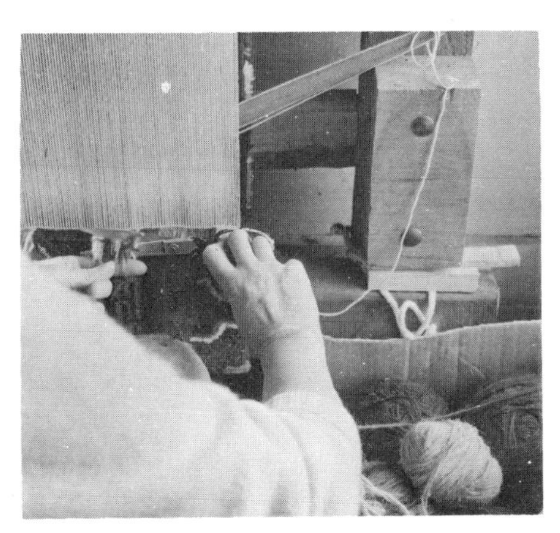

Then the whole row of knots is cut, in either direction, by slicing through the loops at the front of the gauge-rod from one end to the other with a knife. At the same time the weaver pulls the gauge-rod towards her with her other hand to make the cutting easier and smoother. In the days when the gauge-rod was made of wood, it used to have a groove cut along its length to guide the knife. Since modern gauge-rods, being made from pieces of concrete reinforcement or similar metal rod, are not generally provided with such a groove, great care must be taken to cut evenly and in a straight line along the middle of the rod, in order to produce a fairly even pile surface which will need the minimum of shearing.

When the rod is freed from the knots, it is beaten against the warp threads immediately above the completed row, causing them to vibrate and throw off any fluff left on them by the pile yarn while it was being knotted. The rod is then brought down over the cut knots, smoothing them down. All loose ends of yarn are trimmed off with scissors, and many weavers then use the points of the scissors to straighten the pile and disentangle any yarn which overlaps unevenly at the junctions between different colours. Others wait until the final shearing before doing this.

The edge binding is then wound in round the outer pairs and groups of three warp threads, as before. The knotting cycle is now complete. It is repeated a sufficient number of times to finish the carpet, whereupon a further short stretch of end weaving and a final end binding are put in. During the course of knotting, whenever the line being knotted becomes too high up the carpet for comfort, the weaver releases the tension of the loom by removing some of the packing between the breast beam and its pegs, with the aid of the tensioning lever if necessary. She slides the whole warp with its part-completed pile around the warp and breast beams for the required distance, and re-tensions the loom.

Composing the Pattern

Most weavers either know the design of the finished carpet off by heart or are able to compose it as they go along. Often they will copy the design from the back of another carpet which they sling over the top of the loom. If the design is a new one, or is specified in detail by the customer, it is sometimes drawn out full size on paper or white cotton. If this is done, then usually the paper or cloth is marked up into squares about two inches wide, and the outline of the design is drawn in freehand over the squares, which help to guide the weaver's eye. Where complete precision is required, the paper or cloth is marked with much smaller squares, each representing a single knot on the finished carpet, and each square is blocked in with the appropriately coloured ink.

Refinements of Knotting

Many Tibetan carpets, by comparison with those of Central Asia, China, India and especially the Middle East, are coarse in weave and

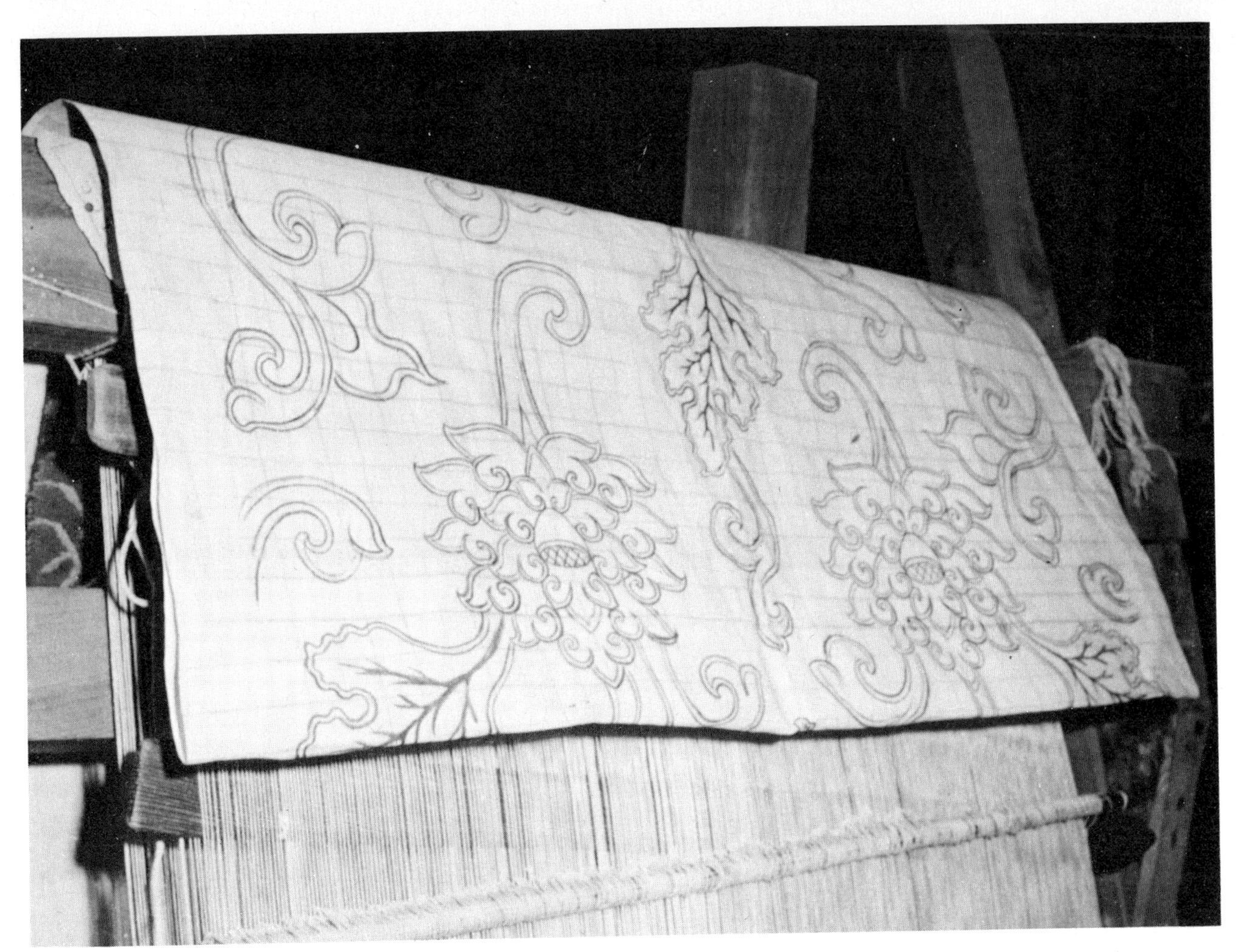

fig. 52 A carpet design drawn out on squared paper and laid over the top of the loom at the Tashi Jong Tibetan Settlement, Palampur.

materials. Their usual range of numbers of knots per square inch, for example, is 40–70 (650–1000 knots per square decimetre), as against more than twice that for high quality Persian carpets, resulting from the thicker warp, weft and pile yarns used. (The method of knotting does not in itself contribute to the relative coarseness. Although each knot is tied on four warp threads, it overlaps its neighbours, so that the effective smallest unit of design is half a knot, occupying two warp threads which is the same space as in most other oriental carpets.) This relative coarseness makes it more difficult to produce intricate patterns with curving lines, since the unit of design, the half knot, is so large relative to the size of the carpet. Partly for this reason, no doubt, many Tibetan carpet weavers have been content to use simple, bold patterns, based on straight lines set at a few limited angles to each other. These patterns may be very pleasing in their own right, but often the weaver wants to create designs of greater subtlety, perhaps copied from a Chinese model. There are a few tricks or refinements of knotting which make this possible.

When starting or finishing a section of knots of one colour, in knotting along the gauge-rod, the loose ends of the pile yarn may be left hanging either above or below the rod, as I have already mentioned. If the line of junction between this colour and the next to the right is to go vertically up the carpet, then the last knot of the first colour, and the first knot of the second colour, are both left with their loose ends

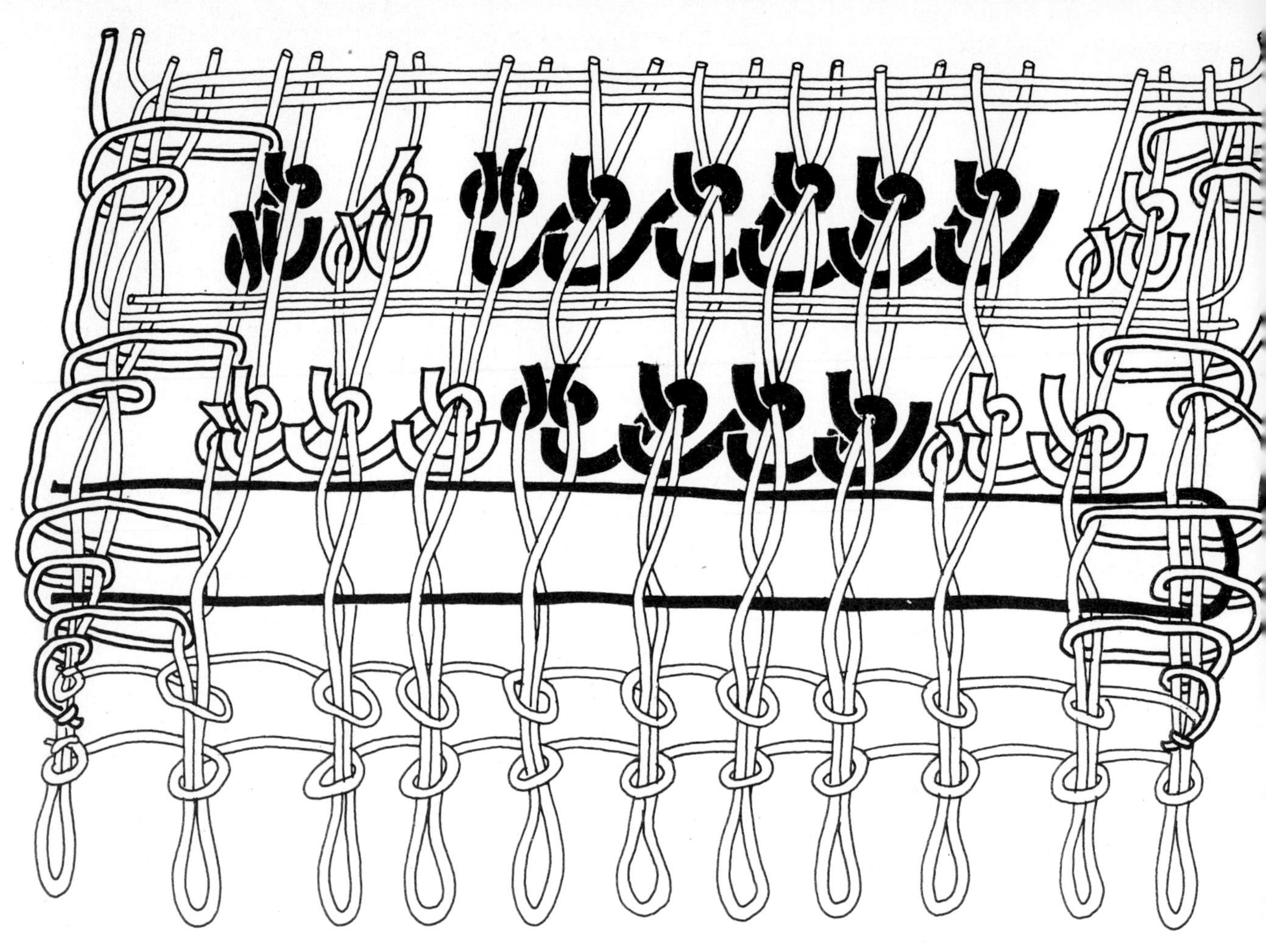

fig. 53 The structure of a Tibetan knotted carpet, showing warp and weft threads, end and edge binding, and pile knots of different colours.

on the same side of the rod, in practice always below. If the line of junction is to slope over to the right as it rises, then the last knot of the first colour is left with its end above the rod, while the first knot of the second colour is left with its end below the rod and vice versa if the line of junction is to slope over to the left. By these means, a slight slope in the appropriate direction is incorporated into the actual junction between the knots within the depth of a single row. The step-like effect which would otherwise be produced by staggering knots in adjacent rows to give a 'sloping' line is thus reduced or eliminated.

Still more subtlety can be introduced into sloping lines by the practice of including an extra warp thread in a knot. This is done in the last knot of a particular section of colour along a row, and has the effect of extending that colour rightwards by the space of a single warp thread, or half a half-knot, at the expense of its rightward neighbour. If there is only one knot of the particular section of colour, the second part of the knot is looped round two warp threads instead of one. Otherwise, the loop is made round three warp threads instead of two.

By this means, the minimum unit of design in a rightward direction becomes the quarter-knot. Although there seems to be no reason why the same effect should not be possible in a leftward direction, by making a knot on fewer warp threads than usual, in practice I have never seen this done. The minimum unit of design in the vertical plane remains the depth of a single row, or two overlapping knots.

After the first such knot with an extra warp thread in a particular

fig. 54 Analysis of the knotting of the segment of carpet shown in Fig. 55.

fig. 55 The segment of carpet analysed in Fig. 54.

row, the following knots, made on the normal number of warp threads, will start on even threads instead of odd ones, and at the end of the row the weaver will be left with only one warp thread around which to make the final loop. She may either make the loop round this single thread, or else 'correct' the row by making at some point along its length another knot on an extra warp thread. Several such knots are sometimes made in the course of a single row. This technique is said by some weavers to be unnecessary on modern carpets with their relatively tight weave and high number of knots per square inch, and seems to be now obsolete.

5. Tibetan *'dzugs*, used as a noun.

A third technique is that of making 'insert' knots ('dzu')[5] between the rows. These are smaller than the standard half-knot in both depth and width. They have the effect either of widening one row at the expense of its upper or lower neighbour, or of providing narrow knots suitable for any sharp points required in the design or both at the same time. An insert knot is put in during the course of knotting the row beneath which it is to go, and immediately before the particular knot which is to go above it. It is made on a single warp thread, one of the set nearer the weaver at the time, whether odd or even, and it is tied from a short piece of pile yarn which is cut off from its ball in advance. The piece of yarn is laid across its warp thread, and each end then pushed under the thread and pulled up from the other side with the fingers. No gauge-rod is used. Insert knots are invisible from the back of the carpet, since the beating of the knots forces them over the front of the weft thread or threads preceding their row of knots.

The late Mr. Aristide Messinesi described initial and final knots of particular colour sections, each made on two warp threads, which I have not seen on either old or new carpets. The initial knot resembles the one I have described above except that the second part of it is made not by looping the continuation of the yarn behind the second warp thread and round the gauge-rod, but by passing the whole ball of yarn behind the second warp thread from right to left and then going on direct to the next knot. There is thus no loop round the gauge-rod to be cut. For his final knot, the ball of yarn seems to be taken from left to right behind the first warp thread, under the gauge-rod, up in front

fig. 56 Shearing a carpet on the loom.

of it and then back behind the first warp thread from right to left. A loop of the continuation of the yarn is then passed from left to right in front of both warp threads, behind the second, from the right, then forward between the two, when it is slipped round the gauge-rod.

Finishing the Carpet

The processes of teaseling, shearing, contouring, tentering, knotting the end fringes and backing the carpet with cloth may conveniently be termed 'finishing'. The first three of these processes were traditionally carried out either as the carpet was being knotted, or on the loom after knotting was finished, with the tension reduced slightly. Nowadays all these operations are often carried out with the carpet flat on the floor.

Teaseling involves scraping the surface of the knotted pile in order to remove as much surplus fluff and lint from it as possible. It is usually done with a 'card' as used for carding wool before spinning—nowadays a flat board about six inches square, with a handle on one edge and many short nails or wires projecting from one side of the surface. This is dragged across the surface of the carpet, removing a surprising amount of fluff. Sometimes a special implement is made by cutting sharp teeth into the edge of a small sheet of steel, and I have seen the job done by dragging the teeth of an ordinary woodworking saw across the surface of the pile. Formerly, weavers used a bone curry comb as employed for currying a horse's coat though I have been unable to find an example of one of these.

In the traditional method of shearing, the axis rod is first removed from all its loops of warp thread, releasing the carpet from the loom. The two ends of the carpet are then joined again by tying together groups of warp threads in bunches, and the carpet is replaced on the loom, so that there is a little tension. The shearer presses the carpet from behind with one hand against the scissors which he holds in his other hand (for no known reason, shearers seem usually to be men). Some weavers prefer to shear short sections of the carpet as they are knotted, reducing the tension of the loom for the purpose and then retensioning afterwards. In the more modern method of shearing, the shearer lays the carpet on the ground, and clips the surface with a large pair of special scissors whose handles rise at an angle so that his hand clears the pile as he cuts. There is a pair of projecting lugs near the points of the blades, which he squeezes with his other hand. Such scissors are used by Indian carpet weavers, from whom this method was doubtless borrowed by the Tibetans.

However skilled the weaver, the pile is never completely even before shearing, for two reasons. First, it is impossible to cut the knots straight along the dead centre of the gauge-rod every time, and second, the projecting ends of cut pile do not stand absolutely vertically (that is, when the carpet is laid on a floor) but slope slightly towards the end of the carpet where knotting began. The purpose of shearing is to convert these irregularities into a surface which is as smooth and level as possible. The smaller the irregularities to start with, the less time is spent in shearing, and the less wool is wasted.

fig. 57 Contouring a carpet.

Once the pile surface is judged to be level enough, it is usually contoured. The idea of contouring is to delineate the pattern on the carpet more delicately by a slight bevelling of the surface along the lines of junction between colours. The shearer first of all makes a cut along these lines of junction with the scissor blades inserted vertically on edge into the pile to clip away any pile threads straying into neighbouring blocks of colour. Then he goes round the whole design again, cutting less deeply and angling the scissor blades to produce the bevelled effect. The operation is highly skilled, especially on the more loosely woven carpets where the projecting ends of pile slope noticeably towards one end. On these carpets the natural slope of the pile can be used to give part of the bevelled effect. A characteristic of some recent Tibetan carpets is the exaggerated and excessive use of contouring. On older carpets the contouring, though an integral part of the overall effect, is hardly noticeable in itself unless especially sought for. On some recent carpets the contouring is not confined to the junction between colours, but extends in the form of shallow grooves cut in the pile within blocks of colour. In extreme examples the carpet is of a single colour, its design existing solely in the form of patterns of such grooves.

Tentering or stretching the carpet so that it is perfectly rectangular and at the same time perfectly flat should only be necessary if the loom was distorted or the weaving inexpert. It is done with a pair of wooden arms up to four feet long, hinged to one another at one end and provided with metal teeth or nails at the slightly wider opposite ends. With the hinge partially open, both sets of teeth are pushed into the pile and downward pressure applied to the hinge, forcing the arms and the sides or ends of the carpet apart. If necessary the carpet may be dampened and the arms held in place for a time by weights suspended from them.

When the carpet is taken off the loom, the 'thrums' or ends of the warp threads at the end where weaving began will take the form of a series of short loops where the warp threads passed round the axis-rod. These loops are often left uncut. The thrums at the other end will also be a series of loops, but unless the carpet is of the maximum length weavable on its loom, which is seldom the case, these loops will be much longer. In this case they are cut to leave a short fringe of single ends. There are various ways of tying the two end fringes into ornamental knots, perhaps the most common being to knot every four thrums or pairs of thrums together in one row of knots, and then every four again in a second row, but staggered so that each knot in the second row has two thrums coming from each of two knots in the first row.

Modern carpets are usually sold at this stage. Formerly they were often backed with cotton cloth or thin felt, usually blue or red in colour. The end fringes were first cut short at the end binding, and the sections of end weaving doubled under the carpet and sewn in that position. Then the backing material was sewn to the carpet along the edge and often down the middle as well. Sometimes strips of thick felt about two inches wide were first sewn right round the edges of the carpet, and the backing material then sewn round these and under the carpet. Occasionally one finds a carpet with felt borders sewn along each end but not at the sides and no backing. All these additions undoubtedly save a good deal of wear and tear on the edge and back of the carpet. They make it difficult to judge the age of the carpet from the smoothness of the back, since it may have been backed and rebacked several times.

A few old carpets are provided with a shaggy woollen fringe all round the edge. This practice has now died out, and I do not know whether the fringe was knotted in during weaving or after the pile was all completed.

Carpet Weaving on the Horizontal Frame Loom

I have not seen this loom in use by Tibetans, but the general principles of its operation may be inferred from the loom itself and from information supplied by Tibetans who have used it. The sequence of operations while knotting and weaving is the same as on the vertical loom; any differences arise from the different nature of the equipment.

I have no information on the precise method of laying the warp and dressing the loom. Before weaving begins, one end of each separate warp thread has been tied round a heading rod and passed between the two parts of the warp beam. The beam has then been rotated to wind onto itself the greater part of each thread, all except a sufficient length to stretch across to the breast beam, where it is fixed by a similar arrangement. Between the two beams, each warp thread passes through one 'dent' or space between two bamboo teeth of the reed, which is supported on the warp threads. The leashes of one heddle frame are attached, half way along their length, to the odd warp threads, those of the other frame to the even threads. The breast and warp beams are tensioned by means of the rods inserted into them.

When performing the Weaving Cycle, the shed and countershed are produced by reversing the relative positions of the two heddle frames, using the pedals, thus raising one set of threads while simultaneously lowering the other. During the Knotting Cycle, all beating, whether of knots or of weft, is done by pulling forward the reed. The heddle frames perform all the functions of the heddle rod and shed sticks of the vertical loom, and the reed those of the mallet and beater-in. The reed is at the same time an effective means of keeping the warp threads separate. As weaving proceeds, the completed web is gradually wound onto the breast beam.

Carpet Weaving on the Backstrap Loom

The principle of laying the warp for the backstrap loom is the same as for the vertical loom; a continuous warp thread is wound round a number of sticks, usually stuck into the ground, three of which correspond to the breast beam, warp beam and axis rod. Sometimes these actual loom parts are used for the job of laying the warp, but sometimes a separate set of sticks, from which the warp is then transferred to the loom parts proper.

The warp beam is tied to a post, pegged to the ground, or otherwise secured, and the weaver tensions the warp by pushing with her legs against the plank, having donned the backstrap. Stringing the heddle and insertion of the shed sticks are similar to the same operations on the vertical loom. At some stage the warp threads are twisted round the laze rod,[6] which normally rests on the top edge of the plank. The warp threads are at their highest point just above the plank, from which they slope downwards on either side to the breast beam and warp beam.

The mode of operation of the backstrap loom is identical in principle to that of the vertical loom, except that the jobs of the mallet and the beater-in are done by the bar-shaped beater-in. This rests in the shed or countershed when not in use, and must be withdrawn and replaced every time the two sets of warp threads are crossed. As on the other two looms, weaving starts at the breast beam. Every time the completed web stretches too far from the weaver for comfort, she loosens the two parts of the breast beam, pulls the warp threads round the whole loom for the required distance, and re-tightens the breast beam.

The Looped Carpet

In discussing the horizontal frame loom and the backstrap loom, I have so far assumed that they are used for making the same knotted carpets as are normally woven on the vertical loom. In practice, any carpets woven on the horizontal frame loom or backstrap loom are much more likely to be of a simpler type, which I shall call the 'looped carpet' to distinguish it from the 'knotted carpet'. The principal difference between the two is that in the finished looped carpet, each separate piece of pile yarn simply passes down behind a warp thread or threads and up at the other side, being in no sense knotted,

fig. 58 Making a looped carpet: the weaver is inserting lengths of pile yarn through the shed.

fig. 59 Making a looped carpet: making the loops round the gauge-rod.

fig. 60 Making a looped carpet: throwing a weft.

fig. 61 Making a looped carpet: cutting the loops.

whereas in the knotted carpet, most pieces of yarn are, at some point or points along their length, twisted right round the threads. A second difference is that in the looped carpet, the pile yarn is looped round only odd or even threads in any one row, while in the knotted carpet it is twisted round odd and even threads together. A third difference is that many of the knots of a knotted carpet overlap each other sideways, while the loops of a looped carpet never overlap.

The making of the loops may be likened to stringing the heddle rod, with the gauge-rod representing the heddle rod, and the pile yarn representing the leashes. Before a line of looping is begun, the warp threads have been crossed over the previous weft. The end of a ball of pile yarn of the desired colour is then pushed into the shed (or countershed, as the case may be) from the right hand side, for as far across the web as that colour will be required. It is then pulled through the near set of warp threads towards the weaver for a short distance and left to rest on the finished portion of carpet. At the point where it leaves the shed or countershed, yarn of the next colour is inserted and pushed along the shed or countershed leftwards, and so on with yarn of all the required colours up to the left hand edge. The lengths of pile yarn in the shed or countershed now form for the moment a discontinuous weft thread right across the carpet.

The next stage is looping the pile yarn 'wefts' round the gauge-rod. Beginning from the left hand edge, a loop of the pile yarn 'weft' is pulled up between each of the upper set of warp threads (corresponding to the nearer set on the vertical loom) and its neighbour, and slipped over the end of the gauge-rod which is moved progressively to the right. Pulling on the loose ends of the pile yarn then tightens the loops on the rod, which now holds the loops as the heddle rod holds its leashes. The gauge-rod and its loops are beaten-in with the reed (on the horizontal frame loom) or with the beating-in bar (on the backstrap loom). A double weft is then thrown and beaten-in. The weft threads are crossed, and the loops cut along the gauge-rod.

With this method of making a looped carpet, the backs of the loops are visible between the weft threads at the back of the carpet. On some looped carpets, the backs of the loops are not visible in this way, the loops being located immediately above the weft threads (when the carpet is laid on the floor). Probably the wefts were thrown before the loops were wound, instead of afterwards, so that the beating-in of the rod and its loops forced the loops over the wefts.

Different Weaves

The above description of the looped carpet assumes that the distribution of warp and weft threads in the basic fabric of the carpet, and of the loops, is the same as for the knotted carpet. That is to say, the warp and weft threads form a plain or 'tabby' weave,[7] interlaced in the regular sequence of 'over one and under one', with a row of loops corresponding to each weft, and one loop corresponding to each pair of warp threads (one odd, one even). In practice, the make-up of a

7. Tibetan *kye-re*.

fig. 62 Making a looped carpet on the backstrap loom. The loops are being made round the gauge-rod. The weaver is a woman of the Thakali people of Nepal, but the same technique is used by Tibetans. She herself sits on a looped carpet.

looped carpet may differ from that model in at least three ways—in the type of basic weave employed; in the number of warp threads around which each loop is made; and in the space left between each two rows of loops. The three examples of looped carpets to be described will illustrate the range of variation.

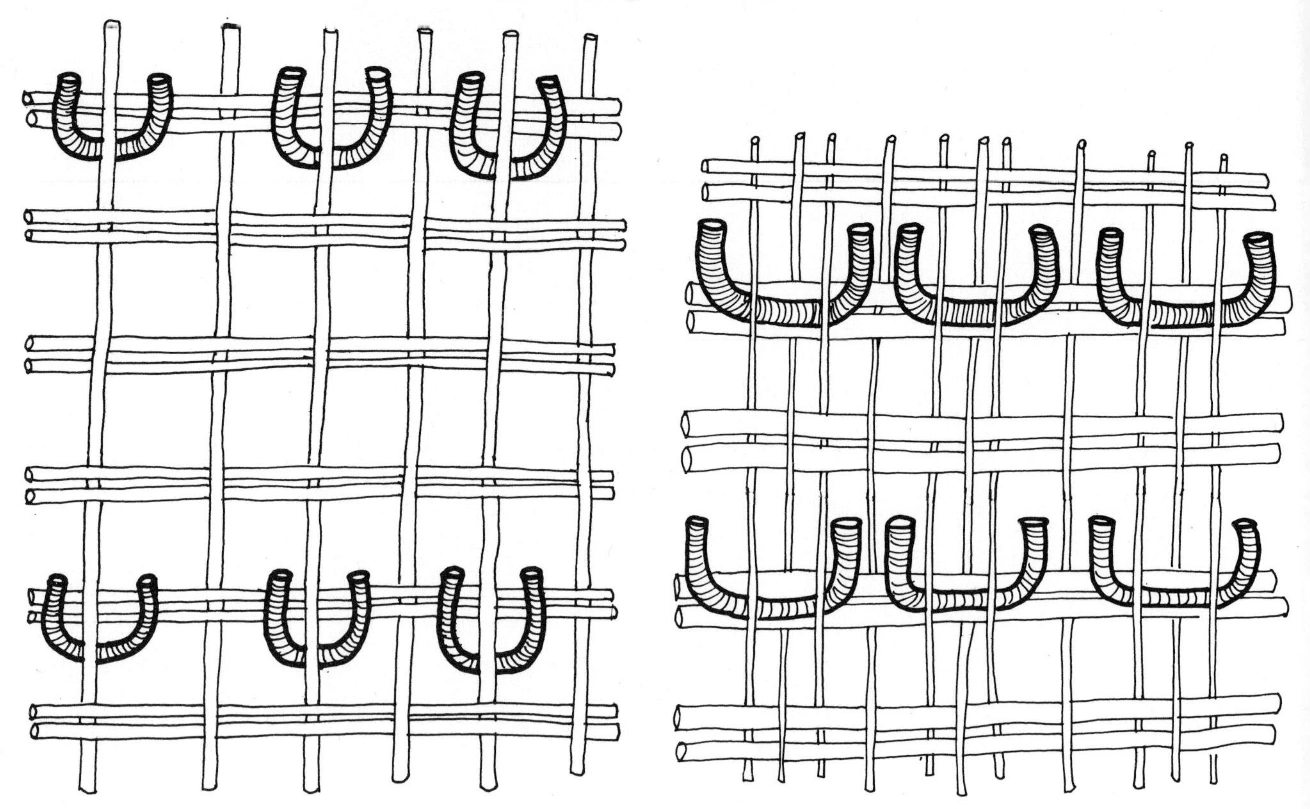

fig. 63 Analysis of part of a looped carpet, type 1.

fig. 64 Analysis of part of a looped carpet, type 2.

In the first example a row of loops has been made only after every fourth weft, leaving three wefts without loops in between every two rows of loops. Since the loops are visible from the back of the carpet, I infer that each row has been made and beaten-in before its weft has been thrown.

In the second example a row of loops has been made after alternate wefts, leaving one weft without loops between every two rows of loops. The weft threads in this example are much thicker than the warp threads and have evidently been thrown before the loops were made, as the latter are not visible from the back of the carpet. Instead of passing round a single warp thread at a time, each loop passes behind a pair of warp threads at a time. Since there is a row of loops for only every alternate weft, all the loops on the carpet are made on warp threads of the same set—in fact, all on even threads.

In the third example the basic weave of the carpet is not plain, but twill[8]; again with a double weft, like all Tibetan carpets I have seen. In this twill weave, each warp thread passes over and under two doubled wefts (four weft threads in all) at a time. The points at which it makes the changeover are staggered one row further up from the points where its leftward neighbour changes over, and one row further down from the points where its rightward neighbour changes over. On the surface of the finished fabric, the raised parts of the warp

8. Tibetan *snam-bu*

threads form ridges running diagonally over the wefts. On this carpet, every two rows of loops are separated by two wefts without loops. Each loop is made round a pair of adjacent warp threads, the left hand one of which will disappear under the weft threads of the next row, and the right hand one of which has just emerged from under the weft threads of the previous row.

To weave a twilled fabric, four different sheds are required, that is, sheds formed by four different combinations of sets of warp threads, a (doubled) weft being thrown once through each of the four different sheds in every four rows. On a backstrap loom, these four sheds are made with the aid of three heddle rods and two shed sticks. The three heddle rods and one of the shed sticks each divide, into two sets, alternate pairs of warp threads (pairs made up differently in each case). The farther shed stick, which is never withdrawn from its shed, separates warp threads nos. 1 and 2, 5 and 6, 9 and 10, etc., from threads nos. 3 and 4, 7 and 8, 11 and 12, etc., the former set being above the stick, the latter set below. The farthest heddle rod may be used to raise the set made lower by the farther shed stick. The middle heddle rod may be used to raise threads nos. 2 and 3, 6 and 7, 10 and 11, etc., and the nearest heddle rod may be used to raise the threads not raised by the middle heddle rod. The nearer shed stick is used to hold all the sheds except that made by the farther shed stick.

To weave a twilled fabric on a horizontal frame loom, an extra pair of heddle frames is needed. This second pair is suspended from a second bamboo pole resting across the upper bars, and is provided with its own pair of pedals. The tie-up is as for the heddle rods of the backstrap loom, except that the farthest heddle frame is tied to the threads raised by the farther shed stick of that loom. When any one of the four different sheds is being held open, the two heddle frames of the pair not involved in that shed are brought level with one another so that they make no shed between them.

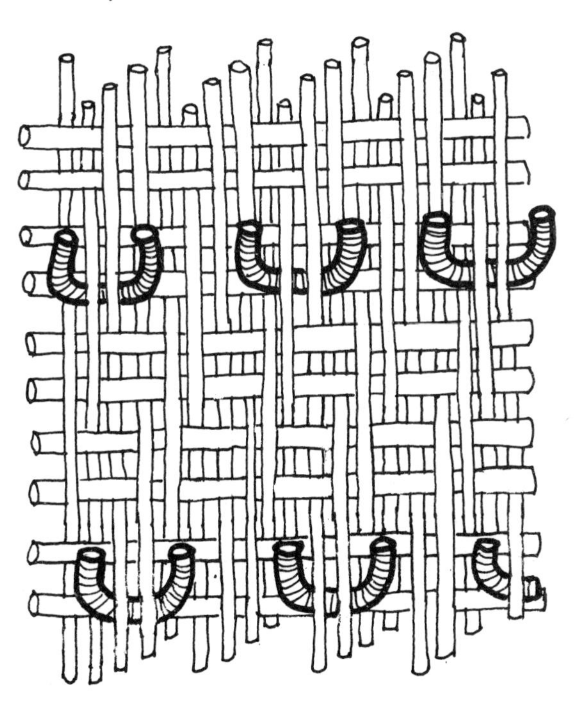

fig. 65 Analysis of part of a looped carpet, type 3.

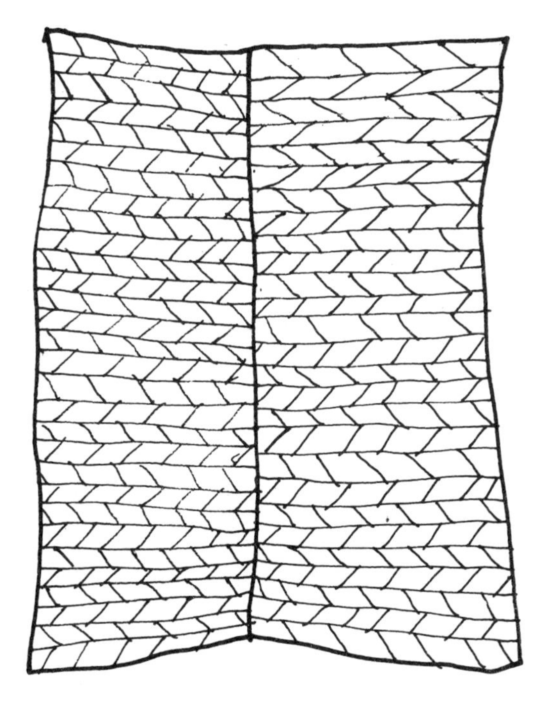

fig. 65a Looped carpet.

Chapter Five
Traditional Carpets

'Traditional carpets' are defined as those made in Tibet proper down to 1959, together with those few made in certain outlying parts of cultural Tibet since then. They may first of all be classified broadly into three main groups according to their mode of manufacture.

Woven Carpets

I shall dismiss woven carpets, if indeed they may properly be called carpets, quickly, since I have examined only one. It was woven in plain weave, with double warp and weft threads, from black yak-hair with two lighter stripes formed by brown warp threads. A somewhat crude meander pattern had been added by binding in white cotton cord, probably after the weaving was completed. The carpet was backed with sheepskin, wool side out.

This type of carpet is mainly used for draping over the backs of yaks and other pack animals, underneath their loads, but it may also be used for other purposes.

Looped Carpets[1]

Plate XXIII, Figs. 10, 65a

Looped carpets are a simple household product made for ordinary household use, especially as bedding. They are usually woven on looms of the backstrap and horizontal frame types. Backstrap looms, and many horizontal frame looms as well, are capable of producing strips of web only about 16 inches wide, with 60 pairs of warp threads at most. Two strips of carpeting made on such looms are generally sewn together lengthwise side by side to make a finished carpet of up to about 32 inches wide by six feet long. For bedcovers and the like, several strips may be sewn together.

The surface of a looped carpet is rough and shaggy, since it is not sheared to anything like the same degree as a knotted carpet, if at all. Slight slippage of the pile loops, which are not gripped so tightly by the warp and weft threads as are the knots of knotted carpets, contributes towards this roughness. When, as is often the case, undyed natural wool is used for the pile yarn, a looped carpet may be mistaken for a sheepskin at first glance. Its precise 'feel' is influenced by the type of weave of the basic fabric, and by the precise disposition of the loops, which, as will be described, vary somewhat from one carpet to another. The number of loops per square inch varies from about 15 to 30. Typically

1. Looped carpets seem to have no standard name. I have heard them called *kha-gdan* and *ma-gdan* by different Tibetans. The word *ma-gdan* is also sometimes used for the lower of a pair of saddle carpets; and in a completely different sense for the ground or field of a carpet.

the looped carpet is soft and flexible, with a loose, open weave. There is none of the springy resilient feel of the pile of many knotted carpets.

Designs on looped carpets vary a good deal, but are almost always simple. Sometimes there are one or more narrow strips across each end, of colours which contrast with the main ground. Some such designs are pleasingly reminiscent of the boldly striped blankets Tibetans make. Often there is a complete self-coloured border surrounding a plain field. Patterns in the field, when there are any, are usually composed of simple shapes made up from squares and straight lines. When arranged symmetrically some of these patterns may faintly recall the medallion designs on the more sophisticated knotted carpets, but often, unrecognisable motifs are scattered apparently at random over the field. They are perhaps the degenerate relics of some formerly recognisable design, or they may simply represent the whims of the weaver. The looped carpet of illustration is covered entirely by horizontal stripes, each stripe being three rows of loops deep and being divided by roughly diagonal lines into sections of different colours.

Fig. 10

The carpet of Plate XXIII is an unusually successful example of a looped carpet whose design imitates one more commonly used for knotted carpets. A 'flower-lozenge' design has been simplified to a linear arrangement in two colours only which can be rendered quite effectively by the coarser technique of the looped carpet. On the whole however the designs on the more ambitious looped carpets are unimpressive, and not to be compared with those of the knotted carpets they imitate.

Knotted carpets[2]*—General Characteristics*

Figs. 66–75

The carpets illustrated in the colour plates, and in Figs 66–75 show the ranges of shapes and sizes of traditional knotted carpets. By far the commonest shape is an oblong, a little more than twice as long as it is wide, and typically 4′6″ to 5′6″ long. Occasionally one comes across much larger carpets, the largest I have seen being 20′× 10′. Small square carpets equal to one half of a normal oblong carpet are fairly common. Saddle carpets have their own distinctive shapes.

The feel and texture of the knotted carpet vary with the quality and nature of the materials used, and with the number of knots per square inch. The latter may be as low as 30, and as high as 80, with 60 a typical figure. By comparison with most Persian and Turkish carpets, all Tibetan carpets are soft, thick and flexible, by virtue of their thicker yarns, looser weave and all-wool construction. The best quality Tibetan carpets have a tighter, denser weave and a thicker, deeper pile, which add a wonderful springiness without taking away much of the flexibility. Undoubtedly the long-stapled and resilient Tibetan wool is important here.

The thickness of the pile varies from about $\frac{1}{4}''$ to $\frac{1}{2}''$ in unworn pieces. Pile thickness may generally be correlated with the number of rows of knots per linear unit of measurement along the carpet, and again with the linear subtlety of the carpet's design. Below about five rows per

2. Knotted carpets are generally called *grum-tse* (sometimes written *grum-ze*) ('trumzi'), or or *rum-gdan* ('rumden'), or just *gdan* ('den'). Sometimes the syllable *rum* is used alone as in the expression *rum 'thagmkhan*, 'carpet weaver'. It also appears in the word *rgya-rum*, 'Chinese-type carpet'. Probably *rum* is a variant of the syllable *grum*, but it is difficult to say what the original meaning of these syllables is. A floor carpet is called a *sa-gdan* ('sapden').

inch the individual rows of knots are clearly visible on the carpet's surface even when it is laid flat, while the rows separate easily as soon as the carpet is bent to make the surface slightly convex. In such carpets the pile is relatively short, and it slopes noticeably towards one end of the carpet (downwards when the carpet is on the loom). Designs in such circumstances have to be fairly simple; these are the bold 'peasant' or 'rustic' carpets. In a carpet with eight to ten or more rows per inch the lines between the rows are invisible and the rows themselves are difficult to separate, while the pile is longer and more vertical. The surface offers the weaver a free hand to create more sophisticated and delicate designs. The feel and appearance of carpets from the extremes of the range are quite different; some idea of the different visual impression may be gained by comparing Figs 68 and 69, and Plate XV with Fig 72.

The three primary colours of blue, red and yellow are lavishly used in Tibetan carpets, for both large and small areas of the designs. All shades of blue are to be found, from very pale to almost black. By comparison with the blues of Chinese and middle Eastern carpets, the Tibetan blues are subdued, and very often streaky and uneven too. The Tibetans seem to have difficulty in getting a brilliant, even shade from indigo, their main blue dye. Perhaps because of this, they make great use of blue as an unobtrusive field colour against which to show off other colours.

Reds may have either a purplish or an orange cast, depending on the dyestuffs used. For larger areas darker shades are preferred, pinks being generally confined to smaller details such as flowers or segments of borders. Yellow is perhaps less used than either of the other two primary colours. The yellow obtained from rhubarb leaves is usually a strawy shade, sometimes with a brownish or even a greenish cast, rather than a rich gamboge.

Of the secondary colours, orange is the commonest. A gingery orange is derived from rhubarb root, other shades resulting from combinations of red and yellow dyes. After the introduction of synthetic dyes a very even medium orange shade became much commoner and invaded the field of many carpets. Green (usually indigo re-dyed with rhubarb leaf) and purple (indigo plus a red dye) were traditionally used sparingly and only for the picking out of small details.

Browns are frequent, especially a buff, 'camel-hair' shade often employed for the field. Walnut and red dyes are often combined to give a range of dark brownish reds. Black is also very frequent for both field and details; it may be natural black wool or natural brown overdyed with indigo and therefore somewhat uneven in depth. White is mainly used for small details.

The Tibetans showed great skill in choosing colour schemes for their carpets. Most of the oldest carpets include yarn of only three or four colours with a dark ground and lighter details. Subtlety and variety are added by juxtaposing different shades of the same basic colour, for instance when the petals of a dark blue flower are outlined with a narrow band of lighter blue, the whole perhaps being outlined in white.

This technique owes much to Chinese textile art. Another interesting technique is that of mixing strands of different coloured yarn in the same knot—the resulting pepperpot mixture of colours can be gradually varied over an area of design to give an effect of shading. As will become apparent, the introduction of synthetic dyes led in many cases to the abandonment of the older canons of design.

Medallion Designs

Plates I–III, Figs. 66, 67, Frontispiece

Medallion carpets, that is, carpets with one or more medallions in a central field, surrounded by a series of borders, are very popular with Tibetans. The finest of them are called 'gyarum' ('Chinese-style carpets'). Medallion carpets as a whole may be divided into three broad types; firstly carpets of predominantly abstract design, usually with three medallions but sometimes only one; secondly carpets with more naturalistic motifs, generally with only one central medallion; and thirdly carpets of coarser weave and less delicate design and colour. Lorentz describes carpets of the third type as being more 'rustic', which is perhaps as good a word as any.

For the first type, a typical succession of borders, starting from the outside, is as follows: edge band, usually in black or dark blue; narrow white stripe; narrow stripe of the same colour as the edge band or of a third colour; wide main border; meander or 'interlocking pyramid' motif (often omitted); dark stripe containing white roundels ('pearl border') bounded to the inside or on both sides by a narrow light blue stripe; narrow white stripe; central field with medallions. Dozens of pieces may be found following this specification exactly and differing only in colour schemes and details.

The pattern in the wide main border is usually made up either of alternating stylised floral sprays and beribboned auspicious emblems, as in Plate I, or of tendril-like scrolls. Occasionally a meander or one of its derivatives occupies the whole main border. The design of the medallions themselves is abstract, though they may incorporate stylised flower-like shapes. The main field is usually dark blue or red, occasionally orange-brown or buff, often, as in Plate I, with small floral sprays, or sometimes individual flowers or clouds scattered around. The four corners of the field may contain triangular corner motifs. Sometimes there is only one medallion, the rest of the field being covered with small flowers or 'water-drop' motifs. Rarely the medallions may be simple frames, containing pictures of dragons, phoenixes or other creatures.

These carpets of the first type are usually refined in taste with delicately though simply drawn designs and a few subdued, harmonising colours, like their Chinese prototypes. Most of them would be called 'gyarum' by Tibetans. The Tibetan colour combinations are distinctive however because the range of natural dyes available to the Tibetans was different from that available to the Chinese; while even in the case of common dyestuffs such as indigo, different shades resulted. The Tibetans make much use of indigo in several shades, of

fig. 66 Medallion carpet.

fig. 67 Medallion carpet cut off just below the halfway mark but showing part of the central medallion. The other half is an almost perfect mirror image of this half. (Entire carpet 72″ × 36″.)

fig. 68 Flower medallion carpet (69″ × 33″).

fig. 69 Flower medallion carpet (59½″ × 33½″).

fig. 70 Flower medallion carpet with medallions of the 'Kazak sunburst' type (72″ × 36″).

madder, lac and madder-lac mixtures, and of rhubarb leaves. Walnut is occasionally used for large areas, but white, green and purple only for picking out small details.

The carpet in Plate I is included as a representative example of the Gyarum type. It is a well-made piece with a carefully delineated design, though it lacks the harmony of the best of its type because of its use of synthetic dyes, particularly a rather vivid red. The carpets in Plates II and III are less typical in formal design but are more beautiful carpets by virtue of their colour schemes and the texture of their wool. Number 2 uses only three dyes—indigo, madder and rhubarb leaf—each in a fairly deep shade most of the time and in a lighter shade for picking out details, with a little green produced by a mixture of indigo and rhubarb and some natural white wool. The balance of shades induces a remarkably restful feeling. Subtlety is imparted to the field by skilful use of the 'uneven indigo' effect. Made of fine, silky wool, this carpet is in excellent condition.

The carpet in Plate III has something of the more 'rustic' feel already alluded to. Bolder and more vigorous than the previous two pieces it is yet the reverse of garish because of the skilful use of a few natural dyes—madder, indigo, rhubarb leaf and walnut. The indigo and madder have their own lighter shades for outlining larger patches of darker shade, while the rhubarb leaf performs this function for the walnut.

Fig 66 shows the medallion design reduced to a simple, geometrical 'rustic' style totally different in effect from the sophisticated Gyarum.

In the second type of medallion carpet, the two flanking medallions are replaced by pictures of recognisable objects, depicted with attempts at perspective and shading to give a more naturalistic effect. These objects are usually bunches or vases of flowers. The wide main border of this type is usually made up of panels of 'Floral lozenge' motifs, alternating either with panels containing more naturalistic flowers or with panels of patterns based on knots and other geometrical figures. A larger number of colours will often be found together on a carpet of this type, many of them synthetic. This fact together with oral information from Tibetans suggests that these designs were not worked out until well into this century, perhaps the 1930s onwards. Part of a very good example (one of a pair) is shown in Fig 67.

Plates IV–VI, Figs. 68, 69, 70

Flower-medallion Designs

These carpets are broadly comparable to the medallion carpets in that three, or sometimes two flowers appear on a central field which is surrounded by borders; but there are many differences of detail and of overall effect. The main difference is that the 'medallions' are in the form of more or less recognisable flowers. They may be divided into three types, all fairly common.

The first of these types has a long black fringe on all four sides. The edge band is black, but much narrower than that of the true medallion carpet. Inside this is a narrow light blue stripe and then a narrow black stripe. The main border is wide, and is patterned like that of the second, more representational type of medallion carpet— often a riot of different floral and geometrical shapes set in separate panels. There follows a pearl border, then a very narrow blue stripe, and then a narrow white stripe. On one example the pearl border is replaced by two bands, the outer one of diagonal stripes and the inner of the 'interlocking pyramid' motif. The central field is buff and is almost filled by three large stylised flower heads from which leaves emerge. On some pieces the flowers are so stylised as to be mere patterns of angular shapes, but on less stylised pieces the flowers are evidently meant to be peonies. The corners of the field are filled with triangular designs made up of mountains, clouds and waves.

Fig 68 shows a fine example of the less stylised kind. The original is done mainly in shades of brown, with a little blue, white and black. A much cruder, coarser and more garish piece is the one shown in Fig 69, of the more stylised variety.

Carpets of the second type have only two flowers, a bunch of leaves taking the place of the central flower. From the two flanking flowers come long, symmetrically arranged branching fronds. The species of flower is indeterminate. The field is some shade of buff, and there may be no border at all. The carpet of Plate V is a beautifully designed and executed piece. It is an outstanding example of the successful use of synthetic dyes, which have been employed for most of the sixteen different colours. I have never seen a similar border on any other Tibetan carpet. On carpets of the third type there is, as a rule, no border, though the example chosen for colour reproduction in Plate IV has a cloud-and-mountain border. Usually the corner motifs of the field present in this piece extend to the corners of the carpet. A small peony bush with a huge single flower springs from the centre of each end of the carpet and a third one from one side, its flower occupying the centre. The field of the pieces I have seen has always been black or red. The carpet of Plate IV is a superior example of its kind, but the flowers have the curious awkward bearing common to the type; angular and yet irregular as compared with the angular stylisation of the first type of flower-medallion design whose angularity is more regular and symmetrical.

The carpet of Plate VI is more idiosyncratic. There are no borders or corner motifs and no awkwardness about the flowers, but the design seems to be related to the third type just described. The flowers still seem to be peonies—two small bats are inspecting their fruits. The orange branches are synthetically dyed, but all the other colours appear to be natural.

Fig. 70 shows a most striking design of three large flowers within a cloud-and-mountain border which does not fit into any of the above three types. I discuss its possible significance for the history of Tibetan carpet designs elsewhere.

As is clearly shown by the pieces illustrated, the various types within the 'flower-medallion' category are quite different from each other in spirit, though by contrast with the 'medallion' category as a whole they all give a much more robust and lively effect.

Plates VII–IX

Lotus Designs

These designs are made up of sinuous stalks bearing leaves, tendrils and lotus blooms, usually arranged in parallel to form a repeat pattern. The basic unit is a stalk shaped like three letter 'S' motifs on top of one another, with six lotus blooms alternatively left and right within the curves. The carpet of Plate VIII, probably an early refugee carpet or one made in the 1950s, has two of these units side by side. As is normal for this design, there is no attempt at overall symmetry, and all the lotuses face in one direction. The outlining of the stalks and petals is typical. Plate VII shows a much older example in natural dyes and includes the top of two units and the bottom of two more. The edges of the carpet do not respect the design but cut across stalks, leaves and flowers. Although the carpet seems at first sight to be a fragment cut from a larger one, I have seen other pieces with similar cut-off blooms which are certainly not fragments. The blue field, red and pink blooms and greenish stalks are usual. The blooms of Plate VII are shown more or less full face, those of Plate VIII in a conventional three-quarter view, again typical for carpets of their respective ages.

The carpet of Plate IX falls into the lotus category rather than any other, but shows some important differences from the carpets of Plates VII and VIII. Here there are four stalk units each with a single bloom, grouped round a central lotus to give rotational symmetry to the whole carpet. The treatment of the flowers is quite different from Plates VII and VIII, though the foliage is similar. Bats do not appear on the other two pieces. I have seen this design with a red field.

None of the three pieces illustrated has a border, though sometimes older examples have a narrow plain red border surrounding the whole carpet.

Branching Floral Design

This design is rare, but authentically Tibetan. The carpet of Plate X is a magnificent example, remarkable for its brilliant and subtle use of natural dyes. The three large orange flowers seem to be derived from the lotus, the two yellow ones, like the leaves, from the peony. The design is symmetrical in colour and shape across its lengthwise axis, and symmetrical in shape but not in colour across its crosswise axis. The slight flaws in the colour symmetry save the design from the lifelessness of perfect symmetry; the same device may be seen on some medallion carpets, for instance that of Fig. 67.

Plates XI & XII

Door Carpets

These carpets are substitutes for the common Tibetan door curtains which are hung over doors to keep out sun and dust while admitting some air. Certain features of the design are representations of parts of cotton door curtains, the broad blue band of the carpet in Plate XI represents the pleated 'pelmet' of the door curtain, as is the band of sloping blue lines on the carpet of Plate XII. The dark blue bands of

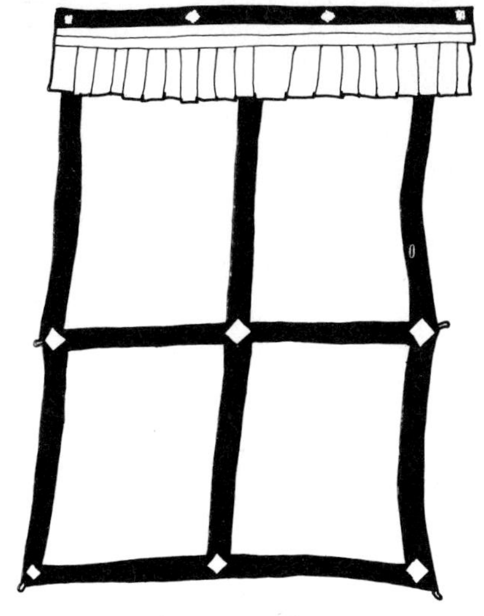

fig. 71 Door curtain.

Plate XII together with the small red squares standing on their corners are normally sewn on to a cotton door curtain from separate pieces of material. The pot and flower motifs which form such a striking part of both carpets is not found in cotton door curtains to my knowledge.

fig. 72 Dragon carpet (54½″ × 33″).

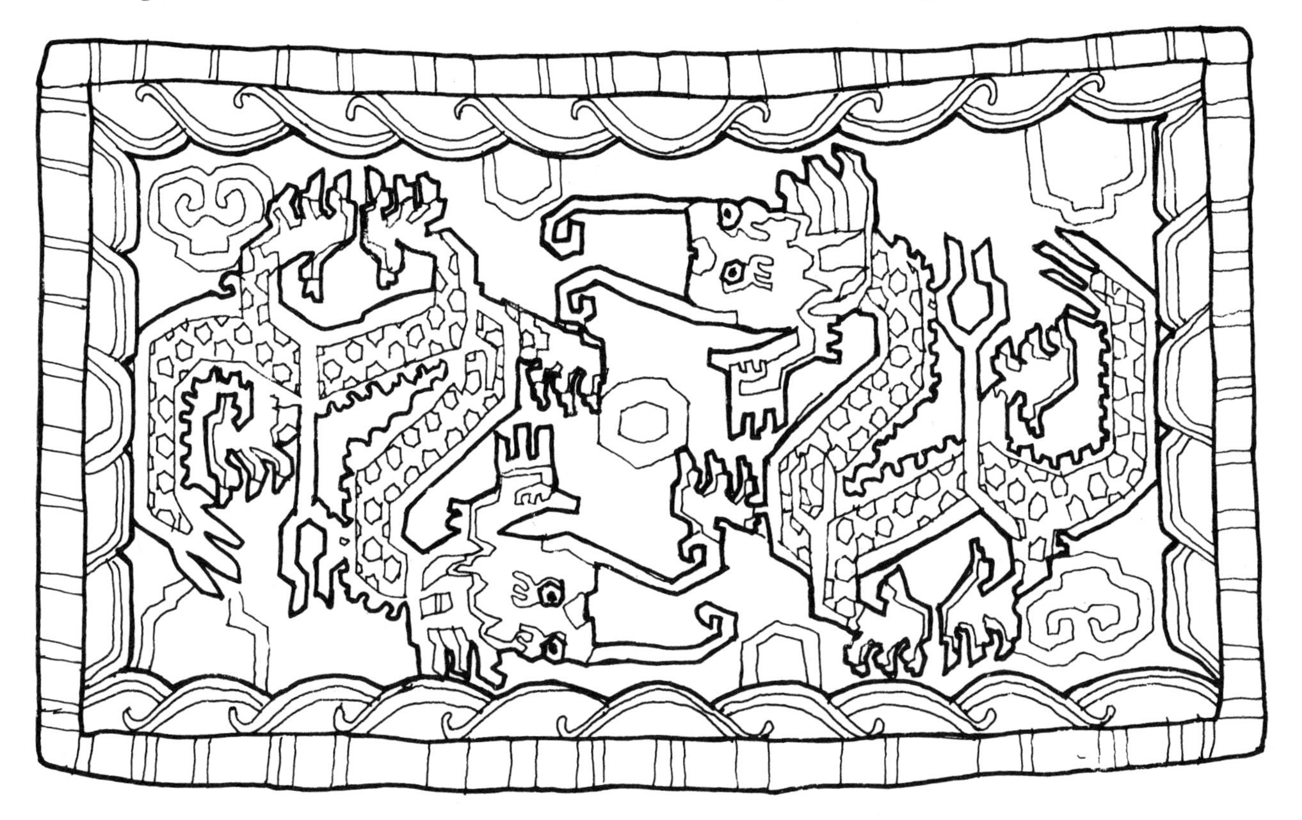

Dragon Designs

Plates XIV & XV

Dragon carpets, including dragon and phoenix carpets, are very popular with Tibetans. The commonest arrangement is one with two sinuous dragons occupying opposite halves of the carpet, facing each other but with their heads at opposite sides, as in Plate XIV and Fig. 72. The two dragons are often of different colours. Frequently there is no border, sometimes a 'mountain-and-cloud' border, as in Plate XIV and Fig. 72. These two pieces show very well the contrast between the

fig. 73 Dragon and phoenix carpet (73″ × 36″).

simple 'rustic' style with coarse weave and the more sophisticated, delicately drawn design with a finer weave. The floating clouds, appropriate to the surroundings of dragons, are usual. A well-known variation is to have a phoenix in place of one of the dragons, with its accompanying lotus blooms. Such is the theme of the carpet in Plate XIII, and older carpet with a fine colour scheme. The dragon is here rather distorted—no uncommon thing on Tibetan carpets.

Plate XV shows a splendid carpet with two dragons and two phoenixes, skilfully delineated, and preserving the rotational symmetry of the carpet in Plate XIV. The carpet of illustration is very unusual in being symmetrical across its crosswise axis. It is one of a pair of carpets made in the Sikkimese royal workshops.

fig. 74 Geometrical carpet, type 1 (59″ × 34″).

Geometrical Designs

Figs. 7, 74, 75

This group comprises two types. The first, exemplified in Fig. 74 has a field divided into small lozenges, each containing a simple stylised flower with four petals. Around the field is a wide border containing a meander which gives an illusion of isometric perspective. In the piece shown, the main field colour is dark red, and there is a continuous fringe round the edge.

The second type is shown in Fig. 75. This also has a field divided up into small units but these, instead of being lozenges, are curious asymmetrical shapes something like arrowheads, again each containing a flower. One piece I have seen has only a simple blue band as border, another has a series of borders reminiscent of the medallion carpets.

fig. 75 Half of a geometrical carpet, type 2. On the other half the design continues without any change in the orientation of the motifs.

Saddle Carpets

Plates XVI–XIX

Saddle carpets form a large and interesting class distinguished by their shape and use rather than by any special design. The Tibetan saddle is made of wood, and considerable padding is needed both between horse and saddle and between saddle and rider. Much of this padding is commonly provided by special carpets, usually one under the saddle and one over it. The carpet going over the saddle is small and rectangular, often with a loop sewn to its underside which can be hooked over the front of the saddle. There are often two cords, one running from front to back of the saddle at each side which also help to hold the upper carpet in place. The lower carpet is larger and distinctively shaped. It is made in two parts, woven separately with what will be the outer ends of the carpet at the bottom of the loom. The two halves are then joined in the middle by a strip of woollen or cotton material.

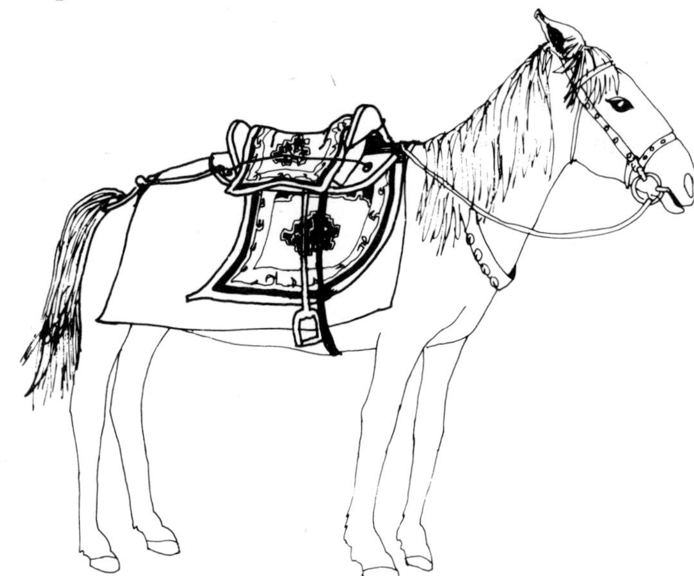

fig. 76 Use of Tibetan saddle carpet.

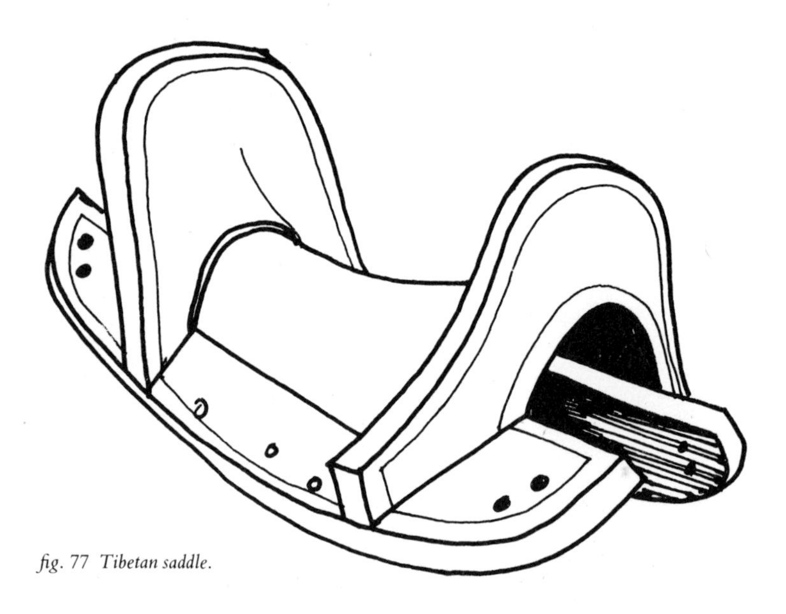

fig. 77 Tibetan saddle.

There are two principal shapes for the lower saddle carpet. The first is shown in Plates XVI and XVII. Each half of the carpet broadens out slightly towards the outer end, and one outer corner, which will be at the back when on a horse, is stepped back. There are two, holes, or sometimes only one, made in each half in the form of slits edged with leather through which the girths are passed.

The second shape is shown in Plate XVIII. The front corners are rounded, while the rear ones flare out to a sharp point. I have never seen a saddle carpet of this shape with holes; the girths pass over the top of the carpet.

The design of saddle carpets is usually based on those of rectangular carpets, but always cleverly adapted to the distinctive shape. On shapes of the first type there is usually room for only one medallion, flower, dragon or other motif on each half. On shapes of the second type one often finds two motifs on each half; in the case of Plate XVIII, a peony flower and a bat. This carpet is unusual in being edged with brocade. The carpet of Plate XIX is its companion.

In parts of eastern Tibet a pair of saddle carpets is sometimes made from two ordinary rectangular carpets. The lower one is used just as it is, the upper one is cut into three with two transverse cuts and the two outer thirds are joined together. Occasionally I have seen lower saddle carpets with rounded, semicircular ends.

Small Carpets

Plates VII, XVIII, XX, XXI, XXII

Apart from the saddle carpets, the pieces so far described have mostly been oblong-shaped, about twice as long as they are wide, and mostly between four feet six inches and six feet long. One often comes across carpets about half this size, roughly or exactly square. Most of them seem to have been made to rest on raised seats. They may be divided into two types; those with a modified version of the larger sized designs, and those with designs rarely if ever seen on larger carpets.

The designs of the larger carpets are usually well adapted to their elongated shape and it would be difficult to fit them into a square format. The most effective method is to use only a part of the design without reducing the scale. Thus a single dragon, single flower or single medallion may be used. The carpet of Plate XXII, though not square, uses a single medallion. It is the personal carpet of a Tibetan lama, which explains its predominantly orange colour.

An alternative to taking part of a larger design for these small carpets is to devise a new design specially for the small size and square shape. Plate XX shows a carpet on which a Tibetan religious practiser sits while performing tantric meditation and ritual. Its field bears a pair of crossed 'dorjes', known as the 'dorje gyadram' (*viśvavajra* in Sanskrit). The dorje itself symbolises the indestructible, adamantine nature of ultimate reality, also the skill in means of the tantric practitioner. In its crossed form it is thought of as constituting the centre and basis of any macrocosm or microcosm, such as the universe, the mandala or mystic circle, or the temple. It is particularly suitable as the seat of a tantric meditator, who in the course of his meditations must identify himself with the mandala and everything it represents. More dorjes are depicted in the outer border, along with human heads and skulls, common tantric emblems, recalling here the practice of meditation in charnel grounds.

The carpet of Plate XXI is another meditation carpet bearing crossed dorjes. The design has been skilfully simplified to suit the coarser weave. These two pieces are good examples of contrasting styles of executing the same basic design.

There are many other designs peculiar to small carpets, too many to illustrate. Very often they depict objects or creatures in a lifelike representational style, for instance, the 'old man of long life', and the 'eight auspicious symbols' of buddhism.

Large Carpets

Plate XXIV shows a rare and beautiful example of a large floor carpet, its central field plain except for four corner-filling motifs. This form of the meander border is unusual. The three classic dyes of medallion carpets: madder, indigo and rhubarb leaves, have been skilfully used together with black. The carpet has apparently been woven in two parts on a standard sized loom, the two halves having then been joined up the middle. Such is not the case with all large carpets, a few of which seem to have been woven on extra large looms.

The carpet shown in the frontispiece is by far the largest Tibetan carpet known to me. It is knotted in fine, soft Tibetan wool on cotton warps and wefts. The design is of the medallion type with the individual motifs enlarged in scale in striking simplicity. Remarkably, it seems to have been woven in one piece. The beige field colour is probably rhubarb over brown wool and the darker brown, walnut. The turquoise colour appears to be synthetic which, together with the cotton base, would date the piece to not more than fifty to sixty years ago.

fig. 78 Carpets for sale in Tsang province 1905.

Development of the Designs

The first crop of photographs of Tibetan carpets dates from the period 1905–10. It is dangerous to argue from negative evidence that designs common in recent times were then unknown, but certainly nearly all the photographs are of non-representational designs with borders—mostly medallion designs. The weave seems to be coarse

fig. 79 Dated photograph showing a Tibetan carpet, taken during an expedition to Tibet in 1911–12.

and the colour schemes simple, and based on a few natural dyes. There is a saddle carpet in the Victoria and Albert Museum, datable to before 1910, with a design and colour scheme very similar to the carpet in Plate XVIII. I would imagine the designs of the carpets in Plates I, II, III, VII, X, XVII and XXIII to be old, that is, 19th century or older.

fig. 80 Formal photograph of Sir Charles Bell with Tibetan dignitaries, the carpet on the floor is of Chinese Turkestan style, 'vase-and-pomegranate design' with a 'cloud-head' border.

The dragon and phoenix design of Plate XIII seems old in style and colour, though probably dragon carpets have had a much greater popularity during this century. They are certainly usually executed in bright synthetic colours, as are 'flower-medallion' designs of the type shown in Plates IV and V.

Chapter Six
Refugee Carpets

The Advent of the Refugees

In the aftermath of the Lhasa uprising of 1959, and in the years following, more than 80,000 Tibetans fled their country for the sanctuary of India, Nepal, Sikkim and Bhutan. Some of them succeeded in finding a niche in areas of Tibetan culture on the non-Chinese side of the frontier, some as traders and shopkeepers in Bhutan, Sikkim or Kathmandu, as monks in Kathmandu or Darjeeling or as farmers in Solu-Khumbu. The vast majority had little choice but to enter the refugee camps set up by their host governments. Numbers of these were set up in the Himalayan foothills, but some were located elsewhere in the subcontinent, as far south as Mysore state. Thanks to generous aid provided by the host governments and international charitable bodies, some of these camps had by the mid 60s been transformed into permanent settlements provided with habitable dwellings, rudimentary health and educational facilities, on the way to self-sufficiency. Those settlements with plenty of agricultural land have generally been the most successful. If a Tibetan family is given the use of a few fields it will quickly make them yield enough, whether for home consumption or sale, to provide a subsistence diet of grain and dairy produce. This gives the family a base on which to build other activities, principally petty trading and shopkeeping, handicrafts and coolie labour. Every autumn hundreds of Tibetans descend from settlements in the Himalayan foothills onto the woollen towns of northern India by buy stocks of woollen goods, mainly sweaters, which they then sell throughout India, hawking their wares in the streets and from door to door. This and similar work is hard and not always pleasant, but the Tibetans understand it and can make very high profits from it. They return to their upland settlements with the approach of the monsoon rains, when cultivation becomes possible. Others may take up coolie labour, mainly on roadbuilding schemes.

In this manner, many of the Tibetans have in a sense recreated their original way of life in a new guise, a way of life based on the large individual family which has a finger in several pies. Many families have become self-supporting and even able to contribute towards small Tibetan monasteries and other manifestations of traditional culture. Attempts to help the refugees by organising larger-scale enterprises such as factory industries and cooperative agricultural ventures have very often been failures. Many of the Tibetans left their country from a dislike of over-organisation and they do not take kindly to some forms of disciplined industrial labour in exile. They are unused to handling and maintaining complex machinery and to the monotony of factory work, or at least they can rarely compete under these conditions with established Indian industries. Carpet weaving, however, is a significant exception to this generalisation. Many of the refugees, perhaps about 85%, were from ordinary farming families in central, southern and western Tibet, perfectly familiar with the idea of carpet weaving and very often with some experience of it. Large numbers came from Tsang province, the centre of the industry, which is within striking distance of the frontier, including several families of master-weavers. The equipment needed is fairly cheap to buy, make and maintain. With no mechanisation, a carpet workshop can be run on a flexible basis with fluctuating numbers of workers—if one suddenly leaves, the whole enterprise is not endangered. The finished product is distinctive and usually of high quality, yet can be sold at prices no higher than those of competitive products.

It is not surprising, then, that carpet weaving workshops were set up in most refugee settlements. A typical such enterprise is housed in a roomy building for the looms, with a small store nearby for the yarn. There may be perhaps a dozen to thirty looms, under the charge of a master weaver and one or two assistants. The weavers are mostly women, who will earn about 80–100 Indian rupees per month at 1974 rates, say £4–£5 or its equivalent. This is a bare subsistence wage under Indian conditions, or, looked at another way, a significant contribution to a family's income. Usually there are nurseries or schools where the children may stay while their mothers are weaving, though small babies very often lie in makeshift cradles alongside their mothers. The atmosphere is relaxed, with plenty of chattering and singing, each weaver or pair of weavers working at her own pace. Nevertheless most of the weavers work quite fast—at the rate of one 6 foot by 3 foot carpet per weaver per three weeks to a month.

Apart from organised workshops, some Tibetans weave carpets in their own homes on a freelance basis, selling them cheaply to other Tibetans, Indians or foreign tourists or using them themselves. A few people treat carpet weaving as a kind of hobby from which a little pin money may or may not be earned.

By now, the Tibetan weavers who actually learned their craft in Tibet are in a small minority. Most of the present weavers were trained in exile under workshop conditions, to weave carpets from a standardised range of patterns, many of them chosen to appeal to foreign buyers, from a standardised and restricted range of materials. Many of the weavers are from families with no tradition of weaving or from areas of Tibet where carpet weaving was entirely unknown. Thus modern Tibetan carpets have taken on some of the characteristics of mass-produced articles and, although still hand made and still distinctively Tibetan, have changed in character considerably, as I shall now describe.

Looms and Equipment

Nearly all refugee carpets are woven on the vertical loom, whose design has in many cases not been modified at all, though it may often be made by Indian carpenters. A standard sized loom may be had for under a hundred rupees, a large one capable of taking a 9 foot by 12 foot carpet, for under a thousand. Any hard, strong Indian wood such as sal pine is satisfactory. Often the looms are fitted with the screwed-on blocks and projecting heddle-bars which I have already described, and occasionally the whole loom is scaled up in size in a way which was probably never done in Tibet. I have only rarely seen the backstrap loom used by refugees—never for carpets. A very few refugees still use the horizontal frame loom for making carpets for their own use.

The 'tak' type of beater-in is now rarely seen, most weavers having gone over to the comb type. Gauge-rods and axis rods are nearly always of metal. Otherwise the equipment has not changed apart from the use of Indian-made knives and scissors.

Materials

The materials of most modern carpets have undergone significant changes in type and quality. In refugee settlements the use of cotton for both warps and wefts is probably universal, though a few private weavers are still using woollen wefts. I have never seen a post–1959 carpet with a woollen warp. Synthetic dyes are now the rule; many settlements buy their yarn ready-dyed in about twenty standard shades from a well-known factory in Amritsar. A few settlements in central India dye their own yarn with synthetic dyes. At least two workshops I know of, one at Darjeeling and one at Palampur in the Kangra Valley, make a point of using natural dyestuffs, though not necessarily traditional Tibetan ones, and Himalayan Indian wool.

The move to cotton for warps and wefts, and the move to synthetic in place of natural dyes, are only continuations of trends already in operation before 1959 and indeed before the Second World War. Developments which began after 1959, or at the very earliest during the 1950s, are the standardisation of carpet sizes and technical specifications and the use of lowland Indian wools. The modern refugee carpet has now been standardised to a remarkable degree. The normal rectangular carpet is nearly always within a few inches of six foot by three foot, with a pile about ½" thick and a knotting density of about 50 knots per square inch (about 750 per square decimetre). In these particulars it is modelled on the best carpets previously made in Gyantse and Shigatse. Another standardised size is about sixteen inches square, suitable for use as a chair cover. A very few saddle carpets are still made for export for use as floor carpets. Some settlements have standardised sizes of seven feet by four and nine by twelve in addition to six by three. While I was staying at the Bonpo settlement at Dolanji there was talk of commissioning a set of temple pillar carpets; in fact most settlements will weave carpets of almost any size and shape to special order.

Designs

Some startling changes have taken place in design since 1959. I shall discuss them under three headings: choice of traditional designs; new designs; and colour and execution.

Of the six traditional designs which I have already described in chapter 6, all forms of medallion design retain their popularity and many new variations on the theme have appeared. Very occasionally it is difficult to tell whether a medallion carpet is old or new at first sight. Of the 'flower-medallion' designs, I have seen the third type occasionally, but never the first two. The 'lotus design', and several kinds of dragon design are still popular. I have seen one carpet in the 'geometrical design' (first type), and none of the 'branching floral design'. Probably no single design, however, is totally forgotten. The Himalayan Marketing Association catalogue depicts a carpet with 'Kazak sunburst' motifs that I have seen on only one old carpet. The carpet shown in Fig. 81, woven by refugees, bears unmistakably 'Khotanese' motifs. Quite likely some of the new designs I am about to mention are in fact old ones which I have never chanced to see on an old carpet.

The new designs which have appeared on refugee carpets are too numerous to describe individually. Virtually all of them are in essence recombination of pre-existing motifs, so that they do retain their Tibetan character even though they depart from tradition. A distinct trend is noticeable towards figurative and representational themes, most of them ultimately Chinese-inspired. Mythical creatures such as the Tibetan snow lion and the 'khyung' (garuda) bird, rarely seen on old carpets, frequently make their appearance. Sometimes carpets are designed to be viewed from one side or from one end, or to be hung on a wall like a picture, something which was formerly rare. The border is omitted much more often than it used to be.

The colours and colour schemes of most modern carpets bear little relation to those of the traditional, naturally-dyed carpets, and often not much more to the carpets which were synthetically dyed in Tibet before 1959. As I have already mentioned, the old naturally dyed carpets used only a few different colours together—usually not more than six. When the Tibetans started to import synthetic dyes they greatly increased their total colour range, but at least they still dyed their own yarns and were able to blend their dyestuffs in many different combinations so that they retained control of the whole process. Nowadays most workshops simply choose their yarns ready-dyed from a sample card which is presented to them. The shades seem to have been chosen fairly arbitrarily, making it very difficult to design a carpet with pleasing colour combinations. Nor are most of the individual colours very pleasing in themselves. The end product is, not surprisingly, very often devoid of the subtlety and harmony of colour which make the old Tibetan carpet such a desirable object. Flat areas of totally uniform colour are juxtaposed with no regard for their mutual relationship. Formerly the wool of each patch or block of colour varied subtly in depth and intensity. The same dyestuff would be used in different strengths and combinations to provide a common factor unifying a particular colour scheme—madder, for example, might be used to dye a pink and a red, at the same time being one of the components of a purple or an orange. In a modern carpet these colours will usually have no such common thread bringing them into harmony.

Although synthetic dyestuffs at first greatly increased the number of colours used together in Tibetan carpets there has recently been a trend towards far fewer different colours, in response to modern Western tastes in interior decoration. Most of the Tibetan carpets are now destined for export to the West, where they may be judged mainly by their ability to fit into some existing or projected scheme of interior decoration. The same markets have induced in some Tibetan carpets the use of more muted or pastel-like shades. Nevertheless, many carpets would better be described as garish in design.

Technically, most modern carpets are extremely well made and finished—probably as well as they ever have been. The standards of composition of the design are not always so high. The best carpets are almost up to the standard of the better old ones, but often the design is clumsily drawn and awkwardly laid out. Contouring is sometimes exaggerated far beyond its original function of delicately sharpening the lines of junction between colours.

I do not want to give the impression that modern Tibetan carpets are not worth buying and studying. Far from it; they are very well made, excellent value for money, usually competent in design, often extremely pleasing and, moreover, are always distinctly Tibetan in character. I would not claim, however, that they are a match for the best Tibetan carpets of forty and more years ago, either in design, colour or texture. It is interesting to compare them with modern Chinese carpets, which have also undergone great changes during this century. The technical competence, the exaggerated contouring and the thick, resilient pile are common to the modern carpets of both the Tibetans and the Chinese. But while a few modern Tibetan carpets share with the Chinese ones a mechanical lifelessness or bland insipidity, most of them retain more or less of that vigour and robustness which the Tibetans put into most of the things they make.

Chapter Seven
The Origins of the Craft

The problems of Chinese Influence

In the preceding chapters of this book I have tried to describe the craft of Tibetan carpet weaving as practised at the present time and in the past few decades. The overall picture which emerges is valid for seventy five years, perhaps even a century back into the past. Beyond that, one has to fall back on informed conjecture. The first problem to consider is the apparently Chinese nature of Tibetan carpets. It has often been asserted that the Tibetan carpet industry is an offshoot or branch of the Chinese. It is easy to see why this view has taken hold. Some Tibetan carpets are virtually indistinguishable in design from Chinese carpets, while the designs of most of the rest are quite obviously Chinese-derived. Other features which many Tibetan carpets share with typically Chinese carpets are their thick, resilient pile, rather coarse weave, cotton backing and felt edging, and contoured surfaces.

Even if this opinion is maintained, it has to be admitted that many Tibetan carpets, though evidently Chinese-inspired, are yet distinctively Tibetan in treatment and colour. However, at least five observations might make one pause before accepting the theory that Tibetan carpets form merely a sub-group of the Chinese, derived entirely from Chinese traditions. Firstly, some Tibetan carpets are obviously not Chinese-inspired, but seem to follow Central Asian or even Middle Eastern models. Secondly, the techniques of Tibetan carpet weaving are quite distinct from those employed in China, as are the equipment and many of the materials used. Thirdly, the craft has developed and thrived in those parts of Tibet that are the farthest removed from China, while it is virtually or entirely nonexistent in the eastern regions which border on China and which have been the most strongly influenced by Chinese culture and products. Fourthly, carpets seem to have been in common use in Tibet for some centuries before the Chinese began to make them, at a time when carpets were regarded in China as mere foreign curiosities. Fifthly, apart from a special class of Tibetan medallion carpets which the Tibetans call 'gyarum' in open acknowledgement of their Chinese models, the Chinese motifs on Tibetan carpets seem to be special adaptations by the Tibetans of designs taken from silks and porcelains and then applied to carpets.

It would seem to be a plausible hypothesis that by about 1000 AD, if not long before, the Tibetans of the Central and Western parts of the country already had a flourishing carpet industry derived most probably either from Central Asia or the Middle East and modified and standardised by themselves and that this existing industry was, from Ching (Manchu) or perhaps even Ming times, subjected to stylistic but not technical influence from China. This influence made itself felt partly through examples of actual Chinese carpets brought into Tibet, partly through the more general diffusion of Chinese art motifs copied from silks and porcelain, and although it bade fair to drive out earlier Tibetan designs, it did not entirely do so.

I shall examine this hypothesis and others in the following sections, pausing merely to point out that because of the scantiness of the sources, it is impossible to reach any very firm conclusions. Little enough is known about the history of Chinese carpets let alone Tibetan. Such questions as where and when the Tibetans borrowed their different types of loom, for example, are quite impossible to answer at the present stage. Some fairly general discussion, however, may help to put the problems in perspective.

History of Carpets in Tibet

Pile carpets have probably been in common use in Tibet for at least the last nine hundred years. The word *gdan* in suitable contexts is fairly common in the literature, although we can never be certain that this refers to *pile* carpets of the modern type. Sarat Chandra Das saw carpets being woven in the 1880s,[1] and western visitors as far back as George Bogle in the 1770s mention in passing seeing carpets in use.[2] The Bonpo text *gZi-brjid*, composed probably in the late 14th century, mentions *gdan* of various kinds in the context of religious arts and crafts. It speaks of 'single' or 'simple' *gdan* bearing designs of *vajras*, swastikas, lotuses, royal wheels or wish-granting gems. These are well-known religious symbols imported along with Indian Buddhism. There are also 'double' or 'complex' *gdan* with some sort of latticework design in a central field surrounded by five-coloured borders, suitable for use by people of official status, and *gdan* of silk or cotton, piled up in three, five, seven or nine layers, suitable for those of royal rank. Again, some form of flexible textile covering is certainly meant but not necessarily pile carpeting.[3]

One of the current words for a pile carpet is *grum-tse*, and when this occurs in old texts we can be fairly sure that a pile fabric is meant. Tibetan lexicographers support this meaning. The oldest instance of its use that I have traced is in the well-known biography of Milarepa, the 11th–12th century saint and poet. When Milarepa was introduced to his guru-to-be, Marpa, he found the latter ' . . . seated on top of two layers of bolster and a carpet (*grum-tse*), making three layers (in all), with cushions, over a floor carpet (*sa-gdan*).[4] From the same work we learn that when Milarepa's mother arranged a feast in her house, ' . . . many carpets (*gdan*) were borrowed and laid out'.[5] Exactly the same happens today in Tibetan communities when anyone is holding a party or other gathering and the passage suggests that carpets were as commonly used

1. Das, pp. 41, 75, 100, 203, 211, 213.
2. Markham, p. 69.
3. *gZi-brjid*, vol kha, chapter 6, ff. 330f.
4. De Jong, p. 56.
5. Ibid., p. 33.

in these parts of Tsang province in the 11th century as they are today. Other facets of local economy seem to have changed little; we read of 'wool-work' as a winter occupation for women; of the fine twill (*snam-bu*) and serge (*ther-ma*) cloths woven in Central Tibet and the Yarlung Valley; of wool being produced by the northern nomads and sold in the 'south' (perhaps Nepal); and of tea and silk being imported through Amdo and Kham. Unspecified dyestuffs are also mentioned.

In the 'Tun Huang' Tibetan manuscripts recovered from the area of the Tibetans' old Central Asian empire, relating to the period of the 8th and 9th centuries, the word *gdan* is attested several times in contexts which suggests that it refers to carpets. Wool, cloth, spinning and felt are also referred to.

Contacts with other Carpet Industries

If the Tibetans did not already have carpets before the 8th century they must certainly have become familiar with them during their occupation of Khotan, Kashgar and other Tarim Basin oases. The Chinese pilgrim Hsüan Tsang recorded carpet manufacture in Khotan and Kashgar in 664 AD.[6] The industry was probably already old there as Sir Aurel Stein discovered fragments of pile carpet at the Lou Lan and Niya sites, other former oases, dating from the 2nd-3rd centuries AD, and also some from Khotan itself.[7] The Tibetans found the weaving of wool, silk and other fibres practised widely in their Central Asian empire and they may well have learned some textile arts from their new subjects. That they were willing in principle to learn is evident from the facts that they invited Khotanese architects and sculptors to work in Tibet and developed styles of painting influenced from Central Asia.

The 8th and 9th centuries were not the only times when the Tibetans had contacts with Central Asia and through it with the Iranian world in which carpet-weaving is of great antiquity. Architectural and agricultural folkways had somehow penetrated to them long before that time. During the 7th century the rapidly expanding kingdom had some knowledge of the Sasanian emperors and of their successors the Arabs. A magnificent silver bowl in Asiatic Greek style, probably made in Bactria around the time of the birth of Christ (and now on display at the Ashmolean Museum in Oxford) must have reached Tibet from the west either through Khotan or via Kashmir.[8] Even after the collapse of the Tibetan empire in the mid 9th century, trade between Khotan and western Tibet contined and was still active in modern times. Russian goods found their way into central Tibet by this route in the 18th and 19th centuries. A few early 20th century photographs of Tibetan subjects include carpets which are either of Central Asian origin or are exact copies of Central Asian carpets, and Tibetan refugees in India are still familiar with a few carpet designs which show unmistakeable Central Asian influence. Probably at no time since the 7th century has trade between Khotan and Tibet been interrupted for long periods. I have seen Chinese Turkestan carpets in the possession of Tibetans; what looks like one is shown in Fig. 7 and another in Fig. 80.

6. Hsüan Tsang's visit to Khotan, and the whole question of Chinese words for 'carpet' are discussed by Bidder, pp. 16ff.
7. Stein, Sir M. A. *Serindia* vol. 1, pp. 242–250, 373; *Ancient Khotan* vol 1, p. 370; *Innermost Asia* vol 1, pp. 229f.
8. Denwood, 'A Greek bowl from Tibet'.

fig. 81 Modern refugee carpet with a design derived from Chinese Turkestan (57″ × 30″).

Tibetan carpets of the 'branching floral' design (plate X) carry a design of flowers and leaves connected by delicate tendrils which is surely related to the well-known 'vase and pomegranate' design of modern Khotanese and other Chinese Turkestan carpets, and to the 'Herat design' often used in the same area. The carpet of Fig. 81 has a single medallion of distinctly Chinese Turkestan type on a plain field surrounded by Khotanese 'cloudhead' motifs in the border. This carpet was woven in exile during the 1960s; it is otherwise quite untypical of traditional Tibetan, or for that matter Khotanese carpets, in employing green as its main colour.

Other carpets seem to take us yet further afield. Those of the second type of 'geometrical design' have their ground covered with a strange, abstract, assymmetrically shaped lozenge motif. I can find no close parallels to this design anywhere nearer to Tibet than in some of the Shirvan and Daghestan carpets of the eastern Caucasus, where similar or identical motifs have regularly been used.[9] A link with the Caucasus is again suggested by a carpet with three bold flower-like medallions which are surprisingly similar to the well-known 'sunburst' motif of the Caucasian Kazak carpets.[10] This motif was occasionally used in Khotanese carpets also. H. A. Lorentz illustrates a rug from Khamba Dzong whose evidently Caucasian design puzzles him.[11] Another of his examples, shown in his Plate 90, must also be placed in this 'Caucasian' category, though it is so unlike any authenticated Tibetan carpet I have ever seen that I am tempted to wonder whether it really was made in Tibet. The knotting technique would decide the point. Since surprises continually turn up among Tibetan carpets, my suspicions may be unfounded.

9. Compare for example the carpets shown in Hubel, plates 46, 56; Lettenmair, pp. 282, 283.

10. Compare the carpets shown in Lettenmair, p. 210; Hubel, plate 43.

11. Lorentz, plate 85, pp. 160f.

As I have already made clear, there is no problem in envisaging the importing of Khotanese and other Chinese Turkestan carpets into Tibet; but what of Caucasian carpets? It is just possible that a few ancient motifs, once widespread over western Asia, have since been wiped out everywhere except in the mountain fastnesses of Tibet at one extreme and the Caucasus at the other. This may have happened with things other than carpet designs. Professor R. A. Stein has already remarked on the curious similarity between some Tibetan and Caucasian styles of folk-architecture.[12] It is perhaps more likely that a few Caucasian carpets were imported into Tibet at some time, possibly by Armenian traders who certainly established a foothold in the country in the 17th and 18th centuries. Although these few carpets are definite evidence of influence from or connections with the west, the classical Persian carpets of the 17th century, which have had such a world-wide influence, have had no discernible effect on Tibet. Nor are there any echoes of the distinctive Turkoman carpets of many parts of Central Asia.

12. Stein, R. A. (II), pp. 9–18.

Turning now towards the east, no contact between the carpets of Tibet and China can be demonstrated before the 19th century, though that is not to say that none existed. The earliest possible time for such contact would be the late 13th century, during the Mongol Yuan dynasty, when carpet-weaving may possibly have been established in a few centres in northern China. There is an unconfirmed report that a carpet manufactory was set up at Karakoram in 1292 to supply the imperial court.[13] H. A. Lorentz can find no direct reference to carpet-weaving in China proper before the 18th century, though he ascribes a few examples of carpets to the 17th. A few state manufactories may have been in operation in late Ming times, the early 17th century, chiefly for the benefit of the imperial court and others rich enough to demand these unusual products of exotic origin. With their customary artistry and technical skill, the Chinese developed their craft to produce superlative carpets in the 18th century, though only in a very few centres. These would naturally catch the eye of any wealthy Tibetan who happened to see them, for the cultural prestige of Manchu China was for the time being high, and fine Chinese products were increasingly in demand in Tibet. Since the Tibetans were already using and making carpets, there would be no difficulty in fitting Chinese carpets into Tibetan houses and monasteries or in persuading Tibetan weavers to copy selected Chinese designs, whether directly from Chinese carpets or from silk and porcelain. The only Chinese carpets copied seem to have been certain types of medallion carpet, faithfully reproduced and called *rgya-rum*. For others, Chinese designs were sometimes lifted straight from porcelain, regardless of whether they were really appropriate to carpets, sometimes readapted and recombined to form new and distinctly Tibetan designs, in every way suitable for the shape and size of a carpet and for the use to which it would be put. This process of copying Chinese models in different ways and at different removes has gone on up to the present day. As I cannot claim any special knowledge of Chinese art motifs, I leave it to others to explore

13. Lorentz, p. 150.

the detailed relationships between the Chinese-derived motifs on Tibetan carpets and their original models.

In modern times carpet-weaving has flourished in the northwestern Chinese provinces of Kansu, Ninghsia (now an autonomous region) and Hsuiyuan (now part of Inner Mongolia), but for three reasons it is difficult to accept the suggestion made by Lorenz that it spread thence to Tibet. Firstly, the craft cannot be shown to have existed there before 1725. Secondly, the designs produced in these provinces show no close stylistic affinity with those of Tibet; the Chinese influence on Tibetan carpets can much more easily be explained by the processes I have outlined above. Thirdly, the neighbouring Amdo Tibetans have not been induced to take up carpet-weaving after the example of these northwestern provinces. To argue for any influence from Kansu carpets to Tibetan we must postulate that examples of them were taken some 1500 miles to the centres of Tibetan civilisation in Tsang. Since far finer carpets were available from elsewhere in China and from Khotan, not to mention Tibet itself, it is unlikely that if any Kansu carpets did find their way to central Tibet, the Tibetans would have been inclined to copy them. Any influence would more likely be the reverse; fine Tibetan carpets taken to Tibetan monasteries in the far northeast of 'cultural Tibet' might well have attracted the attention of nearby non-Tibetan weavers. This carpet industry of northwest China is best explained following Hans Bidder's reasoning, as an 18th century offshoot of the Khotan carpet industry, patronised from the Chinese side and borrowing stylistic motifs from Khotan, China, Tibet and the local peoples. (According to Tafel, some Ninghsia carpets were taken to Tibet in modern times.)[14]

14. Tafel, vol 1, pp. 126f.

The Indian carpet industry is generally reckoned to have been a direct offshoot of the Persian, established under the patronage of the Mughal Emperors. Any influence it may have exerted on Tibetan carpets could not date from before the late 16th century at the very earliest, but from the 17th to the 19th centuries, a few Indian carpets might easily have been imported into southern and western Tibet. Their example might account for some odd floral designs on Tibetan carpets but there is no evidence to show that the influence of Indian on Tibetan carpets was anything but negligible.

Looms[15]

The three looms used in Tibet for carpet weaving and other purposes: the backstrap (frameless), the vertical, and the horizontal frame, are quite distinct and standardised types, giving rise to no hybrid forms. Each of the three clearly corresponds to a major type of loom found elsewhere in the old world, making it possible for us to speculate on the sources from which the Tibetans borrowed their looms.

15. On the history of weaving and types of loom I have drawn on Forbes, Roth, Hoffman, Endrei, Ephraim, Leroi-Gourhan, Schrimpf, Hommel and Pelliot.

Frameless looms have been used in historic times in many areas from Eastern Europe to the Far East, and may be divided into two major sub-types which seem to have been mutually exclusive in any given area; the ground loom of Eastern Europe, North Africa, West Asia and

India; and the backstrap loom of Tibet, parts of China, Korea and Japan, Southeast Asia, Indonesia and Melanesia, and America. The Tibetans are the extreme westerly exponents of the backstrap loom, a type found dominantly in and around the Pacific Ocean. The Tibetan backstrap loom is a very simple version of the type. Similar though not identical forms of it have been used by the Mithei and other peoples of Northeast India, the Dusun and Iban of Borneo, the Igorot of the Philippines, the Ainu of Japan, the inhabitants of some Pacific islands such as Santa Cruz, and various pre-Columbian peoples of Central America. The main differences between all these simple backstrap looms and the Tibetan version is the latter's use of a continuous warp looped round an 'axis-rod' (as on the Tibetan vertical loom), and the foot-plank on top of which the laze rod rests.

Somewhat more developed backstrap looms are known from Bali, Java, Malaya and Cambodia. Their distinguishing feature is a rudimentary wooden frame to hold up the warp beam, which usually takes the form of a flat vertical board. Even more elaborate backstrap looms are recorded from Korea and Japan. These are to all intents and purposes horizontal frame looms, but still with the breast beam held by a backstrap round the weaver's waist, rather than fixed to the frame. At the present stage in our knowledge we cannot say whether these more sophisticated backstrap looms represent steps in the gradual development of the horizontal frame loom from the simple backstrap loom, or whether they are forms of the backstrap loom which have copied some features of the horizontal frame loom. At any rate, the Tibetan backstrap loom is unaffected by such developments, except in parts of Bhutan and perhaps Southeast Tibet. It could plausibly be argued that the Tibetans acquired their backstrap loom at some very early date, probably well before the 7th century AD, from one of their eastern or southeastern neighbours.[16]

16. According to Ephraim, the Buriat Mongols use the backstrap loom. A study of weaving (if any) among the Mongols might help to clear up the question of the 'Mongol carpet' broached both by Lorentz and McMullan. Was there ever such a thing as a 'Mongol carpet'?

The ground loom and its developments never penetrated Tibet, but it is worth discussing briefly because it may have a bearing on the origins of the horizontal frame loom, and versions of it are still used by peoples bordering on Tibet. Its essential difference from the backstrap loom is that both the warp beam and the breast beam are pegged to the ground. Simple forms of it were in use in Egypt by 2,000 BC, while others may still be seen among certain nomadic groups of western Asia. This loom was developed by successive additions which eventually enabled it to perform all the functions of the horizontal frame loom. A pit was dug beneath the warp threads to accommodate treadles, and a separate framework was rigged up from which to suspend heddle frames. Sometimes the warp threads were tensioned by leading them from the warp beam over a higher beam and tying weights onto them. Looms of this type were probably used in Egypt in the 1st and 2nd centuries BC and in Eastern Europe by the early middle ages. Such pit looms are still used in Persia and Northern India, including the Western Himalayas.

The essential features of the horizontal frame loom are the jointed, table-like frame of wood with a seat for the operator and treadles or foot-cords at ground level to operate the heddle-frames. The questions of the origins and spread of this type have attracted the attention of several scholars. Some have argued that it is a purely Chinese development, dating from the period of the Han dynasty, after which time it spread to the Middle East and, by the middle ages, to western Europe, where as the familiar handloom it had replaced earlier vertical types of loom. Others have proposed independent origins in China and the Middle East. It would be out of place to pursue the question in great detail here—besides, much more research is needed. One problem is that no known Chinese loom seems to be an obvious prototype for either the early medieval European handloom or for the Tibetan horizontal frame loom, which two types oddly enough resemble each other much more closely than they resemble any Chinese loom. Chinese horizontal frame looms depicted on stone reliefs of the Han period are of a curiously complicated kind in which a small vertical frame, mounted on top of the horizontal frame, carries the warp. Some later types employ the backstrap principle, usually with a frame which slopes upwards away from the weaver, and a mechanism for raising the heddles which stretches round the far end of the loom. Others have a treadle-pit dug in the ground, rather like Persian and Indian looms, and a complicated superstructure. The heddles always seem to have been raised by rockers. From the point of view of historical development, the relationships betwen the backstrap loom, the horizontal frame loom, and the pit variety of the ground loom have yet to be worked out. There may have been considerable influence and counter-influence between the three types. It is worth mentioning yet another type of frame loom, one found in parts of south-east Asia up to the borders of Tibet, and also cropping up in Kashmir. In this, a high superstructure above the weaver's head is used for hanging most of the parts of the loom except the breast beam. The origins of this type are not known.

While the Tibetan horizontal frame loom may well have been imported direct from China, probably at least five hundred years ago, it seems equally likely that it may have been borrowed from Central Asia or even from some other quarter. Features connecting it with early medieval European handlooms are the extremely simple construction, the horizontal side members, and the use of pulleys instead of the Chinese rockers for raising and lowering the heddles. These features are also shared by certain types of Persian loom still in use.

Vertical looms are known to have been used in many parts of Europe and the Mediterranean coastlands in prehistoric times and in antiquity. They now survive mainly in other regions to which they spread; the Middle East, Central Asia, China and Africa, where they are used mainly for carpet weaving. In Europe they have mostly been driven out by the horizontal frame loom, though the type survives in the tapestry loom. An early form of the vertical loom was the warp-weighted loom, which has a top cross-beam from which the warp threads were hung and tensioned by weights. The weaver stood before the loom and wove from the top downwards. This type, recognisable in classical Greek references, survived till after the Second World War in remote parts of Norway. Another form, the two-beamed loom, has become the usual carpet loom of Western Asia, the Tibetan vertical loom being clearly a version of it, and a very simple version at that. The Tibetan loom resembles in a general way looms used by many nomadic groups and simple villagers throughout western Asia from Anatolia to Afghanistan, though I have not seen any non-Tibetan loom which uses precisely the same principle of separating the breast and warp beams with projecting pegs and packing.

Several observers have discerned three types of oriental carpet loom. In the first, the breast and warp beams are fixed, and the warp threads are simply tied between them. In the second type, the so-called 'Tabriz' variety (which seems to be a usual type among Turkish-speaking populations and in the Caucasus), the breast beam moves up and down for tensioning purposes within slots cut through the uprights and the warp is wound continuously around the breast and warp beams. Thus the maximum length of carpet that can be woven is increased to twice the distance between these two beams. The third type, the so-called 'Persian', has its breast beam and warp beam in the form of rollers held between two vertical ladders. The weavers sit on a plank laid across the rungs some distance above the ground. (A similar arrangement may be rigged up on looms of the 'Tabriz' type). As the carpet is woven it is wound round the breast beam. This classification of looms appears to be very rough and ready, and it certainly needs to be tested against a close study of many actual looms. If it has any validity, then the Tibetan vertical loom approximates most closely to the 'Tabriz' type, in that the warp is continuous and in that its breast beam and warp beam are adjustable vertically but do not rotate.

The carpet looms of China,[17] and also India, seem to direct copies of the more developed looms of both the 'Persian' and the 'Tabriz' types. This is only to be expected, since the carpet industries of both countries are relatively late borrowings, ultimately from Persia, sponsored by the highest levels in society.

17. Lorentz, figs. 38, 39; Hackmack, plate XXVI.

This brief discussion of looms fits in well enough with my previous conclusions that carpet-weaving in Tibet is a folk-industry, using simple equipment, which is at least a thousand years old and thus antedates the carpet industries of both India and China. The nature of the equipment used by Tibetan weavers precludes any direct influence from either country, except possibly in the case of the horizontal frame loom.

Techniques

The Tibetan method of mounting the vertical loom with one continuous warp thread which loops back and forth round an 'axis-rod' is a simple yet ingenious one, whereby an even tension of all the warp threads is achieved with a minimum of work, while at the same time a half-finished carpet may easily be taken off the loom and put back on it without the need to dismantle the whole loom. It is a much better method than those used over most of western Asia, India and China, where the individual ends of the separate warp threads have somehow to be secured to the breast beam one by one, or where the continuous warp thread is simply wound round without any axis-rod. It is not however unique, for T'emurčean describes its use in Armenia.[18] R. G. Hubel assumes that the axis-rod is normally used when mounting looms of the 'Tabriz' type,[19] but most descriptions omit it. H. E. Wulff specifically says that the warp thread is simply led up and down between the breast and warp beams (and on either side of a length of string to form the shed) when this type of loom is mounted in Persia.[20] As I have described already, the Tibetans use the same axis-rod principle in their backstrap looms. I cannot trace an example of any other people using the backstrap loom in this way.

18. T'emurčean, p. 5.

19. Hubel, pp. 25f.

20. Wulff, pp. 214f.

The Tibetan systems of looping and knotting the pile yarn provide important clues for the history of the craft. They are survivals of two very ancient 'cut-loop' techniques called by Louisa Bellinger 'pile made by a weft' and 'Senna Loop', which have long been extinct in the majority of carpet-weaving areas.[21] The 'pile made by a weft' is characteristic of the Tibetan looped carpets in making which the pile yarn is run through the shed and countershed and pulled up in loops round a gauge rod. This is a very ancient technique known in Egypt from the 11th dynasty, about 2000 BC. At first it was used in linen fabrics, but from Graeco-Roman times in Egypt and other parts of the Near East it was used with wool. The 'Senna Loop' is the technique of the Tibetan knotted carpet. Essentially it involves looping sections of pile yarn from a length held in front of the warp threads, behind individual or groups of warp threads, round them and back round a gauge rod. The precise arrangement of the pile will depend on which way the pile is looped, left or right, and round how many warp threads at a time, but it will always differ from what Louisa Bellinger calls the 'Senna Knot' in that neighbouring 'knots' must overlap each other. Variations on this technique were found at Dura-Europos in Syria from the 4th century BC to the 3rd century AD, and in Egypt, where it was

21. See Bellinger.

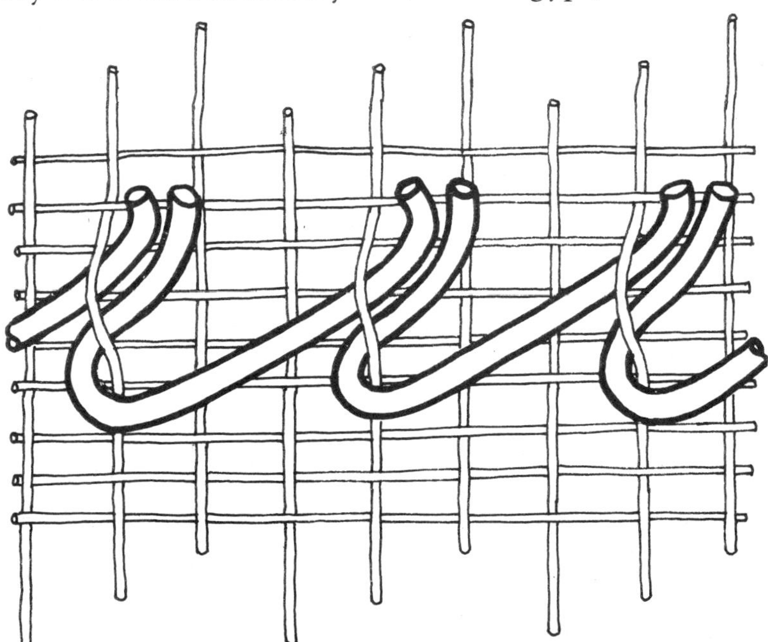

fig. 82 Detail of Senna Loop weaving from Central Asian carpet fragment in the Victoria and Albert Museum (LB IV. ii.00B).

used in a rug of the Coptic period, dated by Dimand to about 400 AD. Dimand considers that pile rugs were made around this time in most parts of the Christian East, as well as in the Sasanian empire of Persia. This empire stretched up to the borders of what is now Chinese Turkestan, where as I have already mentioned Sir Aurel Stein and others found carpet fragments mostly datable to the 3rd–4th centuries AD. Some of these fragments, though not all, are also made by the 'Senna Loop' technique. Thus it is entirely plausible, indeed likely, that the Tibetans should have picked up one or more of these 'cut-loop' methods from Chinese Turkestan during their occupation of the area or even earlier.

These 'cut-loop' techniques have given way in most carpet-weaving areas to the two main types of pile knot, the Turkish (Ghiordes) and Persian (Senna or Sehna), in which individual short pieces of pile yarn are wrapped, not looped, round warp threads. The older 'cut-loop' techniques have died out except in a few peripheral regions like Tibet and Scandinavia where they are still used to make the 'rya' rugs. A cultural connection between Tibet and Scandinavia may sound startling, but it is in no way improbable that textile techniques should have been carried from the near east to Scandinavia, just as they went from the Near East to Central Asia. The Chinese technique of knotting is clearly based on the Persian technique of recent centuries and shows no evidence of any 'cut-loop' system.

Dyeing

The craft of dyeing in Tibet seems to owe much to Persia, although if more were known about Chinese dyeing, connections in that direction might become apparent.[22] Madder and walnut, very common Persian dyes, were widely grown in Southern Tibet; much madder was also imported from the Himalayas. Both Persia and Tibet traditionally imported from India large quantities of Indigo and Lac-dye but few or none of the many other Indian dyestuffs. The Tibetans imported some safflower, a widely grown and used Persian dyestuff, from Kashmir, (although Tibetan authors like many Europeans consistently confused the names of this dyestuff with those of saffron as extracted from a crocus), as well as turmeric, widely used in Persia and north India. In place of other Persian yellow dyes; weld, vine leaves, etc., the Tibetans used rhubarb leaves. They may have learned the use of rhubarb from China, though I have never heard of it being used for dyeing there. Quite likely they adopted it on their own initiative, since rhubarb is a common plant in many parts of Tibet. It is difficult to reach firm conclusions on the provenance of dye plants. The Chinese were familiar with madder and indigo but also used a range of dyestuffs unknown in Tibet. All traceable connections between Tibetan dyeing practices and those elsewhere lead south or west; thus the Tibetans imported dyestuffs in quantity from India, while in Lhasa during the 19th century there were guilds of dyers whose members were Indian or Nepalese. According to Laufer, the Chinese recently imported dyestuffs from Kashmir

22. There is some information on Persian dyeing practices in Wulff and Edwards. Laufer also discusses a number of dyestuffs in relation to China.

fig 83a The 'Coptic' Senna Loop.

fig 83b The Central Asian Senna Loop.

fig. 83c The Tibetan Senna Loop.

via Tibet. Alum and copper sulphate were used as mordants in Persia and India, and a Tibetan recipe for dyeing paper using myrobalan and ferrous sulphate is closely paralleled by a Persian cloth-dyeing technique. Whey, occasionally mentioned in Tibetan dyeing recipes, is also used in Persian dyeing. I hope to return to a more detailed study of Tibetan and other dyeing practices in a later publication.

Conclusions

Bearing in mind the foregoing discussion, my hypothesis is roughly as follows. By the 7th century AD, peoples of Tibetan stock, insofar as it is possible to speak of Tibetans at this early date, had spread from the east as far west as Ladakh, not necessarily to the exclusion of all other peoples in the area. They took with them the simple Southeast Asian backstrap loom which they used for their everyday weaving. As soon as they were in active contact with peoples who shared in the material culture of Western and Central Asia, that is, by the 6th–7th centuries at the very latest, they learned the use of the vertical loom and the basic techniques of carpet weaving which they adapted for use on the backstrap loom and the horizontal frame loom. The latter type they may well have borrowed from Central Asia or by during the time of their occupation of parts of the Tarim Basin, alternatively they may have borrowed it direct from China. By the 11th century carpet weaving was well-established as a folk craft among the villagers and some nomads in western and southern Tibet and it has remained so until modern times. The only major developments since the time of Milarepa have been the massive stylistic influence of Chinese artistic motifs from the 18th century on and the rather more commercialised approach to carpet weaving in a few centres, mainly in the 20th century.

Some remarks of A. Cecil Edwards about the medieval Persian carpet industry might, mutatis mutandis, be applied almost word for word to that of contemporary Tibet;

'These passing references by Arab geographers indicate that the carpet weaving which existed in Persia under the Caliphate was a tribal or rural industry. As such it supplied the needs of the population for a warm, pleasing and durable floor-covering at a reasonable cost. It is likely that the designs in vogue were repeating rectilinear patterns—such as are woven in most of the villages today. They were probably traditional in each locality—as they are today—and they were woven without the aid of designers and draftsmen. This does not exclude the possibility that, here and there, a prince or a member of the landed aristocracy may have possessed a loom or two in his house in charge of a master-weaver; where the lord indulged his sensibilities for the arts by producing something superior to the rungs of the village weavers. This, too, is still a common practice in Persia.'[23]

23. Edwards, p. 3.

Tibetan carpet weaving is essentially a local folk art, derived as such from the Iranian world a thousand years or more ago. Technically it owes little or nothing to the carpet industries of China and India, while developed comparatively late and never reached down to such a popular level. The role of China was to provide the already entrenched Tibetan carpet industry with a wide and highly popular range of visual designs, patterns and motifs which dominate its repertoire to this day.

I

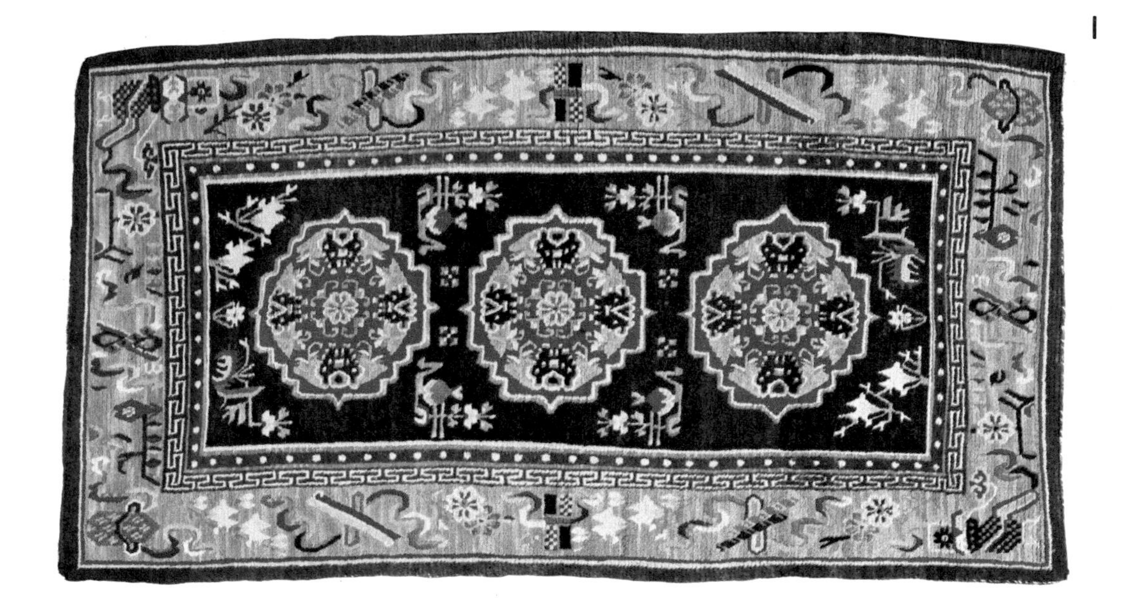

II

III

IV

V

VI

VII

VIII

IX

X

XI

XII

XIII

XIV

XV

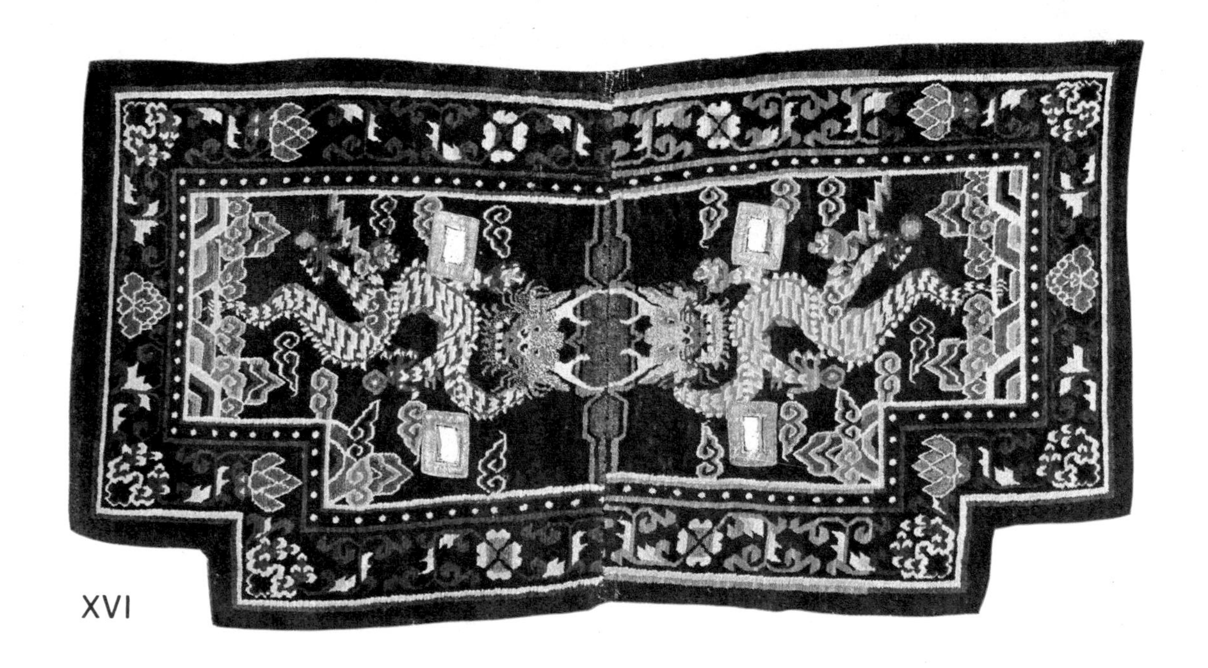

XVI

XVII

XVIII

XIX

XX

XXI

XXII

XXIII

XXIV

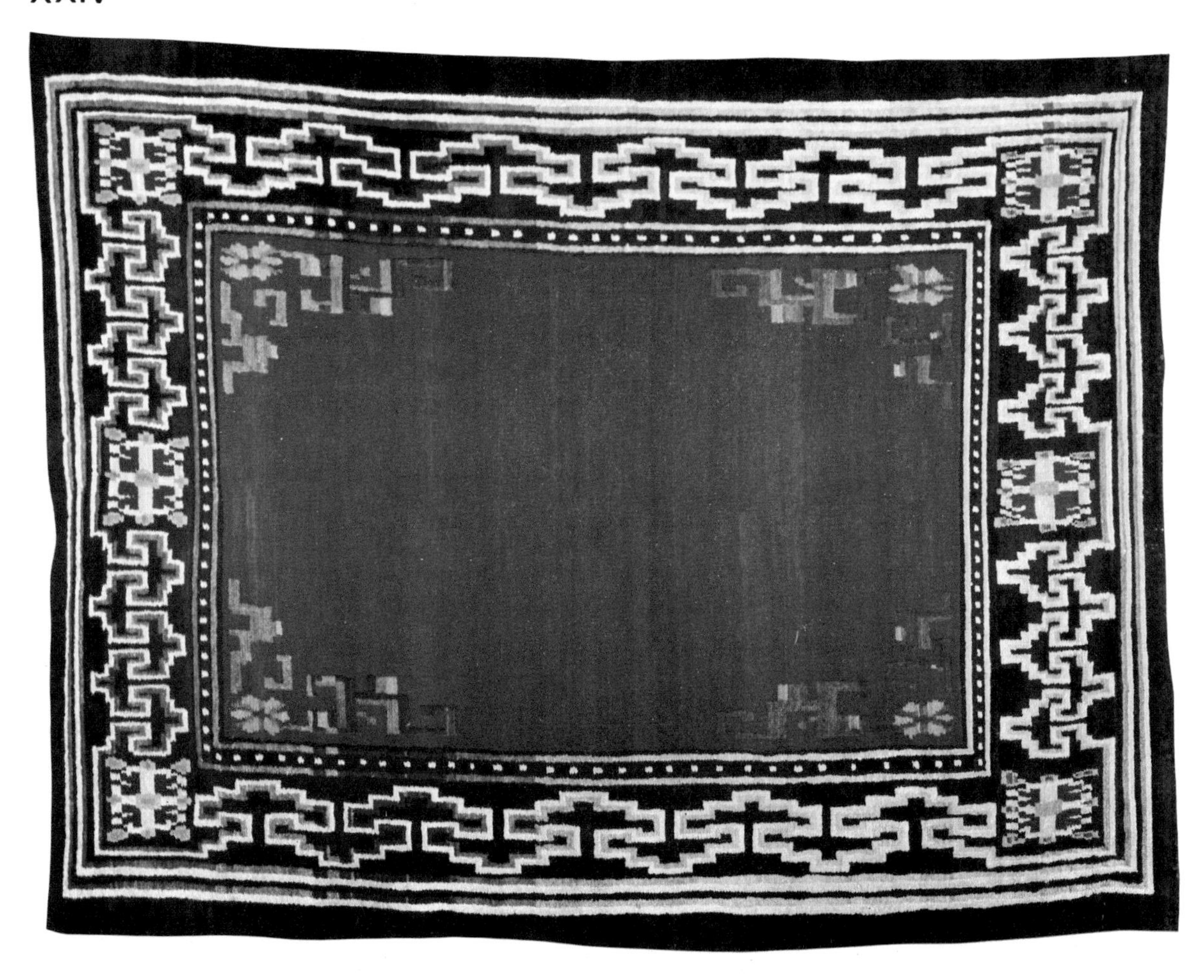

I Medallion carpet
62″ × 36″ (1·58 m × 0·91 m)
Courtesy of Hugh Moss Ltd.

II Medallion carpet
64″ × 30″ (1·63 m × 0·76 m)
Courtesy of Spink & Son Ltd.

III Fringed medallion carpet
60″ × 30″ (1·52 m × 0·76 m)
Collection of Miss Marilyn Silverstone

IV Flower-medallion carpet
71″ × 36″ (1·80 m × 0·91 m)
Collection of Oppi and Saara Untracht

V Flower-medallion carpet
68″ × 36″ (1·73 m × 0·91 m)
Collection of Oppi and Saara Untracht

VI Flower-medallion carpet
65″ × 34″ (1·65 m × 0·76 m)
Private collection

VII Lotus carpet
25½″ × 21″ (0·65 m × 0·53 m)
Private collection

VIII Lotus carpet
64½″ × 35½″ (1·64 m × 0·90 m)
Collection of Oppi and Saara Untracht

IX Lotus carpet
68″ × 36″ (1·73 m × 0·91 m)
Collection of Oppi and Saara Untracht

X Branching floral carpet
66″ × 35″ (1·68 m × 0·89 m)
Private Collection

XI Door carpet
63½″ × 36″ (1·73 m × 0·91 m)
Collection of Oppi and Saara Untracht

XII Door carpet
64″ × 33½″ (1·62 m × 0·85 m)
Collection of Miss Marilyn Silverstone

XIII Dragon and Phoenix carpet
24″ × 30″ (0·61 m × 0·76 m)
Collection of Mr. J. Gelpie

XIV Dragon carpet
72″ × 35″ (1·83 m × 0·91 m)
Collection of Oppi and Saara Untracht

XV Dragon and Phoenix carpet
74″ × 37″ (1·88 m × 0·94 m)
Private collection

XVI Saddle carpet
Collection of Mrs. Jane Loveless

XVII Saddle carpet
51″ × 24″ (1·30 m × 0·61 m)
Collection of Miss Marilyn Silverstone

XVIII Lower saddle carpet
52″ × 32″ (1·32 m × 0·81 d)
Private collection

XIX Upper saddle carpet
29″ × 22″ (0·74 m × 0·56 m)
Private collection

XX Meditation carpet
35½″ × 33½″ (0·90 m × 0·85 m)
Collection of Mr. D. Tremayne

XXI Meditation carpet
30″ × 25½″ (0·76 m × 0·65 m)
Collection of Mr. H. McCoy Jones

XXII Lama's sitting carpet
37½″ × 25″ (0·95 m × 0·66 m)

XXIII Looped carpet
51″ × 31″ (1·30 m × 0·79 m)
Private collection

XXIV Floor carpet
93″ × 72″ (2·36 m × 1·83 m)
Collection of Mr. and Mrs. Adrian Joseph

Glossary of Terms

axis-rod A horizontal rod of wood or metal around which a continuous length of warp yarn is repeatedly doubled back as it is mounted on the loom.
beater-in A tool taking various forms which is used for beating down the weft threads of a carpet during weaving.
breast beam Of the two main beams around which the warp threads pass towards the extremities of the loom, the breast beam is that nearer the ground or nearer the weaver.
contouring Grooving or sculpturing of the pile of a knotted carpet, traditionally along the lines of junction separating different colours.
countershed The space between the odd set of warp threads (to the front, or nearer the weaver), and the even set (to the back, or away from the weaver).
cut-loop technique Any system of carpet knotting or looping in which a continuous length of pile yarn is wrapped or looped into position and then cut to form separate knots or loops.
dent The space between any two teeth of a reed.
dressing the loom Fitting up the wooden frame of the loom with warp, heddle rod and leashes, shed sticks, laze rod etc. ready for weaving to commence.
edge binding Yarn wound into the edges of the carpet at either side of the loom to protect the edges of the finished carpet.
end binding Rows of yarn wound in across the ends of a carpet.
gauge-rod A horizontal rod of wood or metal along which the ends of the warp threads are tied in the horizontal frame loom.
harness A system of cords and sticks connecting the heddle bar and heddle rod in some recent vertical looms.
heddle bar A horizontal wooden bar fixed in front of some recent vertical looms.
heddle frame A pair of thin horizontal rods connected by vertical cords each attached to a warp thread on the horizontal frame loom.
heddle rod A horizontal wooden rod around which the leashes are wound, used for pulling the odd and even sets of warp threads apart.

insert knot A special kind of knot inserted between two rows of normal knots.
knot A single length of pile yarn incorporated in a carpet after cutting, and wrapped completely round one or more warp threads at some point in its length. In Tibetan carpets a single knot most commonly spans two pairs of warp threads, overlapping sideways with each of its neighbours, but it may span anything from one to five warp threads.
knotted carpet A carpet whose pile is made up of knots (q.v.) as distinct from loops.
laze rod A horizontal rod whose job is to discourage warp threads from slipping sideways and tangling together.
lease A horizontal line along which the odd and even sets of warp threads cross and reverse their relative positions.
leash A length of cord or yarn running from a heddle rod, behind a warp thread and back to the heddle rod.
loop A single length of pile yarn incorporated in a carpet after cutting and at no point in its length wrapped completely round any warp thread.
looped carpet A carpet whose pile is made up of loops (q.v.) as distinct from knots.
reed A device resembling a comb with the teeth fixed at each end, used as a beater-in on a horizontal frame loom.
shearing Clipping the uneven face of a carpet's pile to a level, smooth surface.
shed The space between the even set of warp threads (to the front, or nearer the weaver), and the odd set (to the back, or away from the weaver).
shed stick A horizontal wooden stick or slat positioned in the shed or countershed to keep it in being and hold the two sets of warp threads apart.
shuttle A wooden device for holding a supply of weft yarn, passed back and forth through the shed and countershed.
spool The usual Tibetan form of shuttle, being simply a stick notched at each end.
teaseling Scraping the surface of the pile with some toothed implement to clear it of excess fluff and lint.
tentering Stretching the finished carpet to make it lie flat.
thrum The loose end of a warp thread after removal of a carpet from the loom.
warp A collective term for all the warp threads of a carpet or loom.
warp beam Of the two main beams around which the warp threads pass towards the extremities of the loom, the warp beam is that further from the ground or from the weaver.
warp thread An individual thread of warp yarn encountered along any horizontal line across the loom or carpet. It may be a portion of a continuous warp thread or part of a separate thread.
weft A collective term for all the weft threads of a carpet or loom.
weft thread An individual thread of weft yarn encountered along any vertical line along the loom or carpet.

Bibliography

BANCROFT, E. *Experimental Researches concerning the Philosophy of Permanent Colours.* 2nd ed., London 1813.

BEATTIE, M. H. 'On the making of carpets', in: Arts Council, *Islamic Carpets from the Collection of Joseph V. McMullan.* London 1972.

BENEDICT, P. K. *Sino-Tibetan.* Cambridge 1972.

BELLINGER, L. 'Textile analysis: pile techniques in Egypt and the Near East, part 4' *Workshop Notes,* Paper 12. Textile Museum, Washington 1955.

BERTHOLLET, C. L. & A. B. *Elements of the Art of Dyeing.* Translated from the French, 2nd ed., London 1824.

BIDDER, H. *Carpets from Eastern Turkestan.* Translated from the German. London 1964. (German edition *Teppiche aus Ost-Turkestan.* Tübingen 1964.) A very useful survey of this important class of carpets.

CARRASCO, P. *Land and Polity in Tibet.* Seattle 1959.

CASSINELLI, C. W., & Ekvall, R. B. *A Tibetan Principality. The Political System of Sa sKya.* Ithaca 1969.

CHATTOPADHYAYA, K. *Carpets and Floor Coverings of India.* Bombay 1969. Contains useful information on carpets now being woven by Tibetans, Monpas, Bhotias and related groups in India.

DAS, S. C. *Journey to Lhasa and Central Tibet.* Ed. by W. W. Rockhill. 1902. Reprinted New Delhi 1970. A valuable record by a pioneer Tibetan scholar.

DHAMIJA, J. 'Himalayan Region', *Marg* XVIII No. 4, 38ff. Special issue on carpets.

DE JONG, J. W. (ed.) *Mi La Ras Pa'i Rnam Thar. Texte Tibétaine de la vie de Milarépa.* The Hague 1959.

DIMAND, M. S. 'An Early cut-pile rug from Egypt' *Metropolitan Museum Studies* 4, 1933, 151–161.

DENWOOD, P. 'A Greek Bowl from Tibet'. *Iran* XI, 1973, 121–127.

DESIDERI, I. *An Account of Tibet.* Ed. by F. de Filippi. London 1932. Gives a well-informed view of Tibet in the 18th century.

DILLEY, A. U. *Oriental Rugs and Carpets.* Revised by M. S. Dimand. Philadelphia & New York 1959. Chapter IX deals with Chinese carpets. Plate LXX illustrates step by step the knotting technique of Tabriz.

EDWARDS, A. C. *The Persian Carpet.* London 1953. A very full survey of the 20th century Persian carpet industry.

EKVALL, R. B. *Fields on the Hoof: nexus of Tibetan nomadic pastoralism.* New York 1968. An account of the Tibetan nomads' way of life.

ENDREI, W. 'Der Trittwebstuhl im frühmittelalterlichen Europa.' *Acta Historica* VIII, No. 1–2, (Budapest) 1962, 107–136.

EPHRAIM, H. 'Uber die Entwicklung der Webetchnik und ihre Verbreitung ausserhalb Europas.' *Mitteilungen aus dem stadischen Museum für Volkerkunde zu Leipzig* Band 1, Heft 1, 1905.

EPSTEIN, H. *Domestic Animals of China.* Farnham Royal (Commonwealth Agricultural Bureau) 1969.

FORBES, R. J. *Studies in Ancient Technology.* 4 vols. Leiden 1955, Vol. 4 is devoted to textile technology.

GANS-RUEDIN, E. *Modern Oriental Carpets.* Translated from the French. London 1971.

HAACK, H. *Oriental Rugs.* Translated from the German. London 1960. (Original edition *Echte Teppiche,* Munchen 1956.)

HACKMACK, A. *Chinese Carpets and Rugs.* Translated. Tientsin 1924.

HIMALAYA MARKETING ASSOCIATION *Tibetan Handicrafts* (Catalogue no. 2). New Delhi n.d.

HOFFMANN, M. *The warp-weighted loom.* Studia Norvegica no. 4. Oslo 1964. A fascinating study containing much historical information.

HOMMEL, R. P. *China at Work*. New York 1937. Modern Chinese handlooms are illustrated on pages 182 & 183.

HUBEL, R. G. *The Book of Carpets*. Translated from the German. New York 1970.

LARKIN, T. J. *A Collection of Antique Chinese Rugs*. London 1910.

LARSON, K. *Rugs and Carpets of the Orient*. Translated from the Norwegian. London 1966.

LAUFER, B. *Sino-Iranica*. Field Museum of Natural History Publication 201. Chicago 1919.

LAWRIE, L. G. *A Bibliography of Dyeing and Textile Printing*. London 1949.

LEROI-GOURHAN, A. *L'homme et la matière*. Paris 1943.

LETTENMAIR, J. G. *Das grosse Orienttepichbuch* 3rd ed. München-Wels 1969.

LORENTZ, H. A. *A view of Chinese Rugs*. London & Boston 1973. The most thorough study of the subject so far, with many excellent illustrations. Tibetan rugs are included.

MASON, I. L. *A World Dictionary of Livestock Breeds, Types and Varieties*. Farnham Royal (Commonwealth Agricultural Bureau) 1969.

MARKHAM, SIR C. R. *Narratives of the Mission of George Bogle to Tibet, and of the Journey of Thomas Manning to Lhasa*. London 1876. Reprinted New Delhi 1971.

MESSINESI, A. 'Rug weaving in Tibet.' *Quarterly Journal of the Guilds of Weavers, Spinners and Dyers* June & Sept. 1956. Reprinted in Lorentz, H.A, *q.v.*, 124–130.

MCMULLAN, J. V. *Islamic Carpets*. New York 1965. Contains a section with fine illustrations of 'Mongol Saddle Rugs'.

MOORCROFT, W., & TREBECK, G. *Travels in the Himalayan Provinces of Hindustan and the Panjab*. Ed. by H. H. Wilson. 2 vols. London 1841.

OLSCHAK, B. C. 'Tibetan carpets.' *Palette* 27, 1967, 2–11. Well illustrated.

PELLIOT, P. 'A propos du Keng Tche T'ou.' in: Academie des Inscriptions et Belles-lettres, *Memoires concernant l'Asie orientale* Vol. I, Paris 1913, 65–122. Chinese looms are illustrated in plates LVIII & LX.

RAWSON, C., GARDNER, W., & LAYCOCK, W. *A Dictionary of Dyes*. London 1901.

ROPERS, H. *Morgenlandische Teppiche*. Braunschweig 1955.

ROTH, H. L. *Studies in Primitive Looms*. 3rd ed. Halifax 1950. Covers many parts of the world. His 'Bhotiya' looms are of the Tibetan type.

SCHRIMPF, R. et al. Entries on 'Tissage' in *Dictionnaire archéologique des techniques*. 2 vols. Paris 1963.

SCHUETTE, M. 'Geographical Distribution of Tablet Weaving.' *CIBA Review* 117, November 1956. pp. 9–18.

SCHÜRMANN, U. *Central Asian Rugs*. Translated from the German. Frankfurt an Main 1969.

SCHUTZENBERGER, M. P. *Traité des matières colorantes*. Paris 1867.

SHAKABPA, W. D. *Tibet. A Political History*. New Haven and London 1967.

SNELLGROVE, D. L. & RICHARDSON, H. *A Cultural History of Tibet*. London 1968.

STEIN, SIR M. A. *Ancient Khotan*. 2 vols. Oxford 1907.

STEIN, SIR M. A. *Innermost Asia*. 4 vols. Oxford 1928.

STEIN, SIR M. A. *Serindia*. 5 vols. Oxford 1921.

STEIN, R. A. (I) *La civilisation tibétaine*. Paris 1962. (English edition *Tibetan Civilisation*. London 1973.)

STEIN, R. A. (II) 'L'Habitat, Le Monde et les Corps Humain en Extrême-Orient et en Haute Asie'. *Journal Asiatique* CCXLV, 1957, pp. 37–74.

SYLWAN, V. *Woollen Textiles of the Lou-Lan People*. Stockholm, 1941.

TAFEL, A. *Meine Tibetreise*. 2 vols. Stuttgart 1914.

T'EMURČEAN, V. S. *Gorgagorcut'yune hayastanum*. (Carpet weaving in Anatolia) Erevan 1955.

TIFFANY STUDIOS. *Antique Chinese Rugs*. New York 1908. Reprinted Tokyo 1969.

TUCCI, G. *Tibetan Painted Scrolls*. 3 vols. Rome 1949.

TUCCI, G. *Tibet, Land of Snows*. London & New York 1967.

WEIR HARDY, J. *Tibetan Carpets. Method of Weaving & Design Symbology*. New Delhi (Himalayan Marketing Association) n.d. (c. 1968).

WULFF, H. E. *The Traditional Crafts of Persia*. Cambridge, Mass. & London 1966.

Index

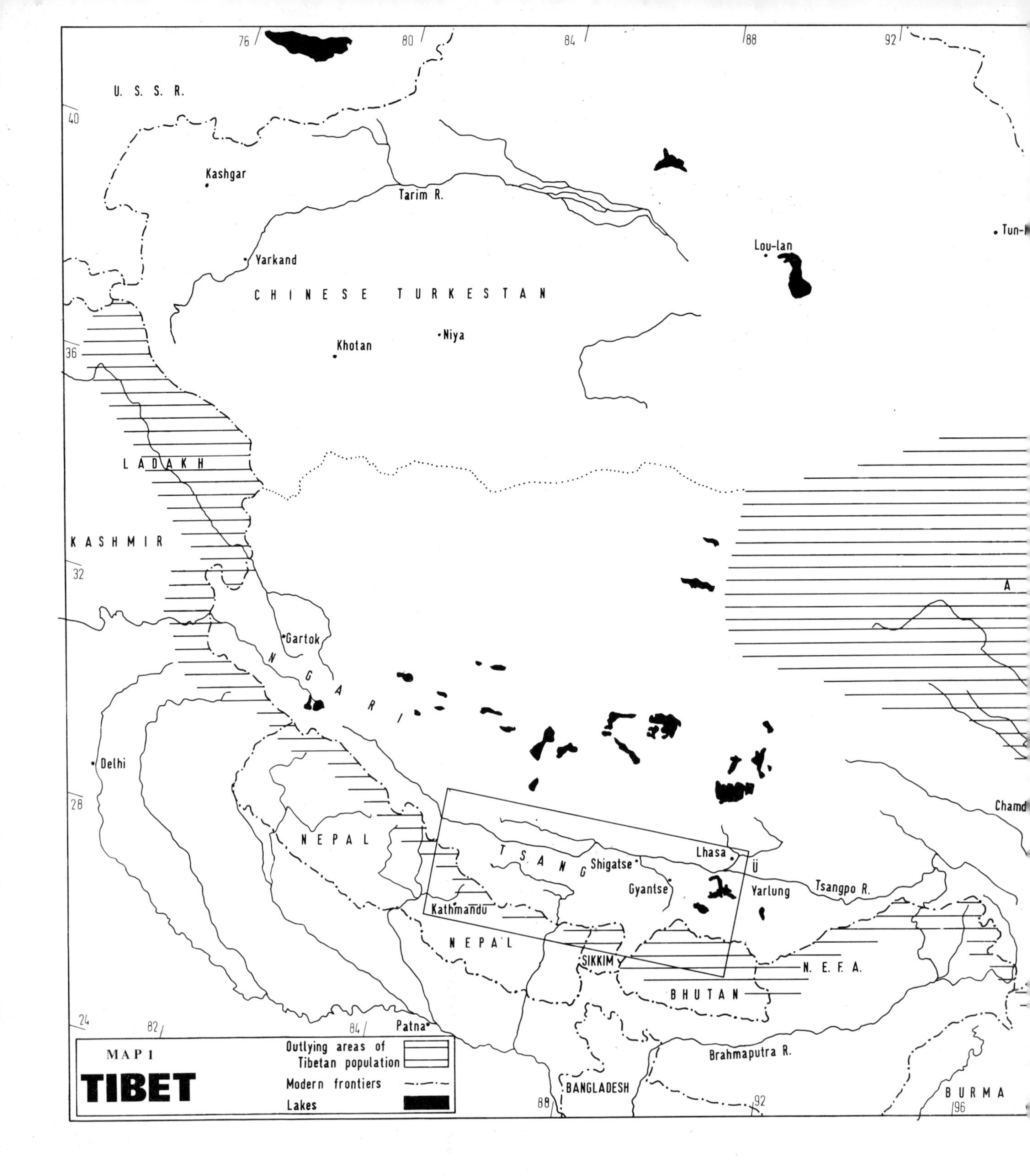
U. S. S. R.
Kashgar
Tarim R.
Yarkand
CHINESE TURKESTAN
Khotan
Niya
Lou-lan
Tun-
LADAKH
KASHMIR
Gartok
NGARI
Delhi
NEPAL
TSANG
Shigatse
Lhasa
Ü
Gyantse
Yarlung
Tsangpo R.
Kathmandu
NEPAL
SIKKIM
N. E. F. A.
BHUTAN
Chamd
A
Patna
Brahmaputra R.
BANGLADESH
BURMA
76
80
84
88
92
40
36
32
28
24
82
84
88
92
96
MAP 1
TIBET
Outlying areas of Tibetan population
Modern frontiers
Lakes